Reaching for More
our story of abandoned expectations and a life renewed through the Holy Spirit

CHUCK AND MARIANNE SNEKVIK

DEDICATION

To Ingrid. Our beautiful daughter, wife, mother and lover of God.

And to Amy and Andrew. May your names be a blessing. We are grateful for the years we had with you. What a privilege! We miss you both terribly, but we'll see you again soon.

INTRODUCTION

For over fifty years, we have been telling stories that introduce people to Jesus.

We started on college campuses in the 1960s, talking to students about the God of the Bible and who He claimed to be.

Throughout our life together we've accumulated our own stories. Each story we tell says something about who God is.

First and foremost, God is good. God gave us exciting work to do, deep connections in Christian community, and three beautiful children.

But our stories also tell of the risky world God allows us to live in. We were blindsided by tragedy that forced us to abandon our expectations. We learned that while God does not condone evil in the world, He doesn't always stop it either.

Our stories also tell of the messes we get ourselves into because of our free will. Driven by grief, anger, and past hurts we hadn't forgiven, we acted in ways that pushed us apart from one another.

In our most desperate moment, we learned that God has more for us. It took a renewal to teach us how to let go to God's Holy Spirit. When we did, we found healing in our marriage. We also found renewal in our faith.

We have lots of wild stories about what God can do when we let Him work through us. We witnessed miracles of healing all around the world. We experienced miracles of inner healing within ourselves, also helping countless people find freedom through extended prayer. And we learned that God is always there, always ready to love us, and always waiting with more.

We are ordinary people sharing our story of God's extraordinary love. We hope our stories will encourage you. We hope you will read this and ask God for more of His love and all that God has for you.

EARLY LIFE

GOD CREATED THEM, MALE AND FEMALE
(GENESIS 5:2)

Our (Chuck and Marianne) early lives set the scene for our future relationships. Like most parents, ours did the very best they could. But in differing ways, our fathers and mothers let us down. We each came to adulthood with hurts from the past that colored our relationship with God and with each other.

It would take years for each of us to undo the hurt of childhood. Eventually, God taught us how to forgive our parents. In time we came to see that God is a more loving, more perfect father than any person could ever be.

CHUCK: My parents had me in the middle of WWII, 1942. They gave us a comfortable home in Seattle. I grew up the oldest of 3 children in a family that went to church every Sunday. In the Ballard neighborhood of Seattle, everybody we knew went to church faithfully at the Ballard First Lutheran Church. I loved the songs we sang together there. I loved being around other people singing to God. On the outside everything was picture perfect. We were close to our cousins. My dad led my Boy Scout troop. I really enjoyed tying knots and earning merit badges, but mostly I loved backpacking and making fires. Our family loved hiking, camping and boating on Puget Sound. My dad attended my sporting events, and I loved

1

playing catch with him in the backyard.

I always wanted to please my dad, but he had a short temper. In his eyes, I could never get it right. If he wanted a Philips screwdriver, I might hand him a flathead. He would explode in anger and say, "What's the matter with you?" It made me cringe when he spoke to me like that. And yet I still wanted his approval. In the back of my mind I resented the fact that my mother couldn't protect us from my father's anger.

The thing I wanted most was to go hunting with my dad. He had all these hunting friends in Seattle, and I remember looking enviously at their equipment before they set off on a trip. They laid everything out - all the packs and camouflage protection and knives. I desperately wanted to be a part of it. I often asked my dad, "When can I go hunting with you?" He always said, "When you get older." So, I waited to get older.

Just before I started high school we moved from Seattle to northern California for my dad's job. We left all our friends – everyone we knew – and it was a big shock to everyone in the family.

One day not long after we moved, I was out walking with my dad. I remembered about the hunting trips he used to take with his buddies, and I said to him suddenly, "Hey, I'm old enough now. When are we going to go hunting?" My dad turned to me kind of surprised. He got a sad look on his face. "We're not going hunting," he said. Who would he go hunting with? All his friends were in Seattle. Just like that, the hunting trip was off the table. In that moment something in my heart gave up. I still wanted affirmation, but I stopped trying to get it from my dad.

I stayed angry with my dad for a long time after that. Once I expressed that anger when we were playing a game of touch football. I tagged my dad, and I pushed him extra hard. It was only supposed to be a touch football game, but I nearly slammed him down onto the concrete. My dad looked at me and said, "You did that on purpose." I couldn't say anything back to him. He was right. I had done it on purpose.

In the years I've spent pastoring and helping people connect with God, I've often had to remind people that our earthly fathers are not always the best model for God.

God is always good, and He always love us. He wants to "give good gifts to those who ask Him," as Jesus says in Matthew 7:11.

But our natural fathers don't always do this. My dad didn't give me the love and affirmation I asked for. He hurt me with his anger. It took me a long time to realize how much this affected me. It colored my relationship with God. I spent years seeking the approval of a powerful church leader, and I developed anger issues myself. I was stuck in a place of believing I wasn't enough.

A long time later I forgave my dad and learned to experience God's unconditional love. But I'm getting ahead of my story here. Even in my early days, God was with me step by step. We moved to California, and although the move was hard on me, it brought me into the same state as another special person. This person would change my life more than anyone else (other than Jesus, of course). I'm talking about my future wife, Marianne.

MARIANNE: I was born and raised in California – the baby of my family.

When I was two years old, my oldest brother was killed in World War II. It was a terrible shock to my parents. My brother's plane was shot down and his body was never recovered. After that, my parents didn't have much interest in God or in church. They were nice people, but church just wasn't their thing.

My dad drank to deal with his feelings. I never saw him drink at home. I just remember many evenings when he wouldn't come home after work. My mom would have his dinner waiting in the oven while we ate. She'd say, "Oh, he got involved with somebody after work, and they went out for a drink." It was always supposed to be just one drink. But once he got started, he didn't come home for a long time. I'd be waiting up in bed, unable to relax and go to sleep until I heard him come home.

At the time I didn't verbalize any of my feelings. But I think I internalized the message, "I don't really matter." If I mattered, my dad would have come home to eat dinner with us. Since he was out drinking, I must not have mattered to him.

Much later in life, when I got involved in church, I learned that God really does love us, even when we don't feel it. Jesus even prayed to God saying, "you love them as much as you love me" (John 17:23). But for the first part of my life, spiritually speaking, I was pretty much on my own.

3

My dad worked for the Union Oil Company of California, and job transfers meant that we moved every couple of years. After one of our moves, our new neighbors invited me to go to church with them. My parents didn't mind, even though they didn't want to go to church themselves. So, I went to church with the neighbor and she took me to the Sunday school classroom.

In Sunday school I asked a lot of questions. The teacher was impressed with my eagerness to learn about God. She said to me, "Would you like to stay later and learn more about Jesus?" I did. That day the teacher led me through a prayer of inviting Jesus into my heart. I remember how excited I was to tell my mom when she picked me up in front of Eagle Rock Church in Burbank!

"Mom! I invited Jesus into my heart today!"

"Oh, that's really nice," my mom said.

"Hmm," I thought. "That's odd." All the other people at the church had been so excited for me. I guess my mom doesn't really care about this God stuff.

I went to church a few more times, but after we moved again, I didn't get back into religion. I drifted around spiritually, being an bratty teenager who was often mean to my parents. I didn't get excited about God again until my last year in college.

As a college senior, I lived with a few girlfriends in an off-campus apartment near UC Berkley. Downstairs from us were three guys who were involved in Campus Crusade for Christ, a campus Christian ministry, now known as CRU. They kept inviting me and my roommates to go to their meetings, and we kept saying no. But these guys were persistent. They just kept asking. Finally, I said, "Okay, I'll go! Just to get you off my back!"

I went to my first meeting, and I was surprised. It wasn't boring at all like the church services my parents disdained. The meeting was held at the home of the Campus Crusade head staff person at Berkeley. It felt like just a bunch of nice people hanging out. They talked, they sang songs, and they had refreshments. Everybody seemed really normal. Actually, they seemed better than normal. They seemed great. They seemed like people I wanted to hang out with more. The next meeting was a big event for all the students on campus. I went to that meeting and loved every minute of it.

I don't know what exactly changed in me over the course of a few short meetings. But it wasn't long after that my parents drove down to visit me from Sacramento. They picked me up from UC Berkley, and together we drove out to see my aunt, who happened to be the one person in my family who had strong Christian faith. When we got to her house, my dad pulled my aunt aside and asked, "What's happened to Mary? She's done nothing but talk about God ever since we picked her up!" To my aunt's great joy and my parent's confusion, I was hooked on Jesus.

At the end of my senior year, one of the Campus Crusade guys sat me down for a talk.

"Marianne," he asked, "What's the most important thing you ever learned here at college?"

"Well, I guess that Jesus forgave everything I ever did. And that I could have a relationship with him," I said.

"So, what are you going to do next with that most important piece of information?" he asked me.

That seemed like a good question.

When I thought about it, I realized I wanted to help other people come to know Jesus. So, at his prompting, I decided to get trained to spread the gospel to other college campuses.

And that's where my story intersects with Chuck's.

MEETING AND FALLING IN LOVE

A MAN LEAVES HIS FATHER AND MOTHER AND CLINGS TO HIS WIFE (GENESIS 2:24)

We met and fell in love at a very exciting time. It was the 1960s and everything was changing around us. On the college campuses where we worked, God was moving in a powerful way. A lot of new believers were coming to Jesus. Young people felt they had more power than they'd had at any other time in U.S. history, and we felt important and useful to God. We were consumed with our work and had no desire to get married. But God had other plans for us.

God literally threw us together, over and over again, often in humorous ways. When we got the message that we were meant to be a together, we jumped into our marriage with both feet first. We were young, impulsive, and excited to give the rest of our lives to God.

CHUCK: After high school in California, I returned to Washington state to attend Pacific Lutheran University (PLU)! In college I'd had my own plan for what I thought was best for my life. I took a year off and I went to Europe on an "educational tour," or at least that's what I told the draft board. In reality I was a ski bum. When I returned to PLU my junior year, I was a man of the world. I was a leader. In fact, I took the lead in

6

organizing all the keg parties. I went to a Christian school, but it sure didn't look like Christ was the center of my life.

During the summer break between my junior and senior years at college, something happened that changed my life. All the PLU students living in California got invited to a big party in Santa Cruz. In reality it was a Christian conference, but my brother and I drove down in his little red TR3 convertible with every intention of meeting girls and having fun. Inside the conference, I listened out of one ear while I scanned the crowd for girls I might want to talk to.

At one session, the speaker was talking about what it meant to follow Jesus. Out of the blue the guy asked, "By the way, how many of you are Christians?"

Almost every hand went up.

My brain stopped suddenly when I heard that question. Up until that point I had assumed I was a Christian. My family went to church. I had been confirmed. I even went to a Christian university! But for some reason, his question hit me like a ton of bricks.

"How many of you are Christians?"

I was 22 years old and there was no part of me that could raise my hand and say, "Yes, I'm a Christian." I went outside and took a walk by myself. I was all shaken up inside. It was the moment of decision that people talk about, but I had never faced. Would I be a Christian? Or not? That day I gave my heart to God in a new and sincere way, choosing to follow Jesus.

I went back to PLU to start my Senior year. I was hanging around with the same crowd of beer-drinkers, having a good time like I always did. Once when I was talking tough and swearing up a storm, one of the guys turned to me and said, "Chuck, I thought you found Jesus. What's going on?" He was right. What was going on with me? I had been changed inside but I had to get changed outside too.

I still kept hanging out with my old friends but found new ones too. One of my new friends started to disciple me – to train me in how to follow Jesus. We would read the Bible together, pray together, and talk about our lives. One day he said, "We should go to Bal Week to tell other people about Jesus." I said "sure!"

Bal Week was short for the Spring Break celebration at Balboa Beach in California. All the Christian students who were involved in college ministry would go down to Balboa beach to talk to the students there about Jesus. We jumped into my Volkswagen and drove to Southern California.

While down there we met a large group of students from Texas. They invited us to go with them on their bus to the Campus Crusade headquarters.

We boarded a bus filled with 50 of the best looking girls and guys you'd ever seen. These impressive Christians would break into spontaneous songs. One person would start singing *In God's Green Pasture*, and they'd all fill in with perfect two-part harmony. I thought I'd died and gone to heaven.

After I went back home I was reflecting on the whole experience. I wanted more of what I experienced that week, one of the best I'd ever had. So, I signed on for a leadership training camp with Campus Crusade over the summer.

And that's where I met Marianne.

The first time I saw Marianne, it was across a dorm room that was so small I couldn't fit inside. I stood in the doorway waving hello as my buddy introduced me around. It wasn't until a few days later that Marianne and I got to talk for real. I was walking down the path in the middle of campus that led to and from the student center, the place where you picked up your mail and bought snacks and sodas. As I was leaving the student center, Marianne was walking up the path to go to the student center. Since we had been introduced a few days earlier, we both stopped halfway to talk to each other.

I had just picked up a snack of peanuts and my bottle of soda. As I remember it, it was a normal fun conversation. But Marianne remembers it differently. In her mind, something funny happened. Marianne says that as I was talking to her, I started dropping the peanuts into the bottle of soda. Then I drank the soda, peanuts and all. That sounds weird. I don't remember doing this, and I've never done it since. I guess God just wanted to give Marianne a message: if you stick with this guy it's going to be different – sweet, salty, sparkling and surprising all at the same time!

Marianne and I had a fun time talking. We felt really comfortable with one another. All through that summer our relationship developed as friends. At one point I borrowed her car to take another girl to Disneyland. Meanwhile, Marianne would talk to me about guys she thought were cute. We both took staff training that summer. At the end of the summer Marianne was assigned to the University of Oregon, and I returned to PLU as student staff. I was jazzed. We had weekly meetings and formed teams to share Jesus with everyone on Campus.

By January I was assigned to Oregon State University.

As staff, we would go out into all the hang-out spots and invite people to our once-a-week meetings. At each meeting, somebody from Campus Crusade would stand up and give a little talk about God. Then we hung around and chatted. "What did you think of the message?" we would ask the kids. "Would you like to talk more?" If they were interested, we'd make appointments to meet for coffee in between classes. We learned more about their lives. And we talked to them about Jesus.

We also went into sororities and fraternities and gave talks there. We had a memorized speech that explained Jesus in a simple and compelling way. "He claimed to be one with God," we would say. "So, Jesus had to have been either a liar, a lunatic, or Lord. He didn't give you any other choices." Was Jesus deceptive, crazy, or was he truly God? We'd ask the students what they thought. If they conceded that Jesus might be God, we'd ask, "So, would you like to get into a relationship with him?" We prayed with many people. After they turned their lives to Jesus, we'd keep meeting with them. We got them reading their Bible and growing in the Christian life.

One of the students we worked with was Dick Fosbury who later won a gold medal in the high jump at the summer Olympics in Russia. His coach told him he could never win a gold medal by using his unique technique of going over the bar backwards. After he proved his coach wrong and won Gold, everyone now uses his technique.

After the summer staff training, I left to finish my last year at PLU, and Marianne worked as campus staff at the University of Oregon. Over the course of that year we saw each other a few times. We both attended regional meetings of Campus Crusade staff. On New Year's Day, Marianne and I drove together to the Rose Parade in Pasadena, California with a truck full of pre-packed lunches to hand out. During that long ride to the Rose Parade, there was a flicker of something between us. Maybe we were becoming more than just friends.

There were other trips between Oregon and Southern California. Once my friend and I gave Marianne a ride in my little green Volkswagen Bug. We guys kept Marianne laughing all the way from San Bernardino to Sacramento, and not just because my friend was 6' 3" and could barely fit in the front seat. Then there was a long conversation in a coffee shop near UCLA after we had spent the day talking with students in sororities and fraternities about Jesus.

Talking to each other about the work we both loved so much, Marianne and I held each other's gaze a bit longer than normal. For a moment we both thought, "Hmm. Maybe there's something there." But for the most part we weren't looking for love. We were caught up in the work we were doing.

Campus Crusade was a cutting-edge ministry in those days, and we felt like we were on the forefront of what God was doing. We were jazzed about meeting kids on college campuses and bringing them into a relationship with Jesus. Both Marianne and I loved the work. We loved talking about God, and we loved seeing what God was doing for other people. It was during our second summer of Campus Crusade leadership training that Marianne and I both got assigned to the University of Oregon in Eugene. Actually, God threw us together. Literally threw us together. It happened in a blue Cutlass.

At that time everyone in Campus Crusade was raising money to buy a car, and the Cutlass was the car to buy. One staff member had a red Cutlass, and another had a white Cutlass. I had a brand-new blue Cutlass, and another staff member had an identical blue Cutlass. When we all met for weekly staff meeting, there were four Cutlasses lined up out front. They were bright shiny examples of God's goodness to the Campus Crusade staff.

One morning my roommate and I picked up Marianne in the blue Cutlass to go to a staff meeting. I was driving, Marianne was sitting in the middle, and my roommate was in the front passenger seat talking about the book of Job. He had just gone to a conference where they talked about Job, and here he was going on and on about trusting God through trials and tribulations. Suddenly, out of the left-hand corner of my eye I saw a blue Cutlass shoot out at us. This blue Cutlass was owned by a Campus Crusade staff member named Jesse James. He was a real life descendent of the outlaw Jesse James. And that day he drove like an outlaw, too! There were no stop signs on those back streets, so technically I had the right of way. But Jesse James didn't stop. He slammed right into the driver's side of my blue Cutlass, knocking us to the other side of the road.

My car smashed into the curb, and I got smashed up against Marianne. That was the sign – God literally throwing us together. When we got out of the car Marianne said, "My hip hurts." I said, "Let's get out and get the blood moving." I didn't know that when I crashed into her I had broken her hip!

The police officer arrived at the scene, and he thought we were trying to pull one over on him. Here were two identical blue Cutlasses, bought off the same dealership in Detroit, with license plate numbers that only differed by one digit. Both had insurance policies made out to Campus Crusade. And what's more, the guy at fault in the accident said his name was Jesse James! The officer thought we were a bunch of smart alecks.

Soon after, Marianne and I were both assigned to work for Campus Crusade on the campus of Oregon State University in Corvallis. During the week we would stay with a family near the university. Then for the weekend we would drive back to the University of Oregon to join the staff team. We were spending more and more time together, driving back and forth for meetings. We also met for coffee most days to compare notes about our work with students on campus.

One day while driving Marianne back from Corvallis in my Volkswagen Bug (my Cutlass was getting repaired), I realized that I wanted to hold her hand. Her hand was right there on the console next to mine. And I wanted to hold it. It was a 60-minute drive to Corvallis, and I started slowly moving my hand towards hers. It took me about 30 minutes to get my hand over to where hers was, and another few seconds to get up the nerve to drop it on top of her hand. When I did, she didn't pull her hand away! Wow! That was an exciting moment. A short time later we went on a date together to see the Tijuana Brass. It felt like we were walking on air with each other – well, at least I was – Marianne was still hobbling around on crutches because of her broken hip.

For a little while, nothing big happened between us other than that one date and holding hands in the car. The turning point came all of a sudden one night after a Campus Crusade staff retreat.

That evening we were sitting around a big table with a whole lot of people. I was at one end of the table, and Marianne was at the other. Everybody was talking, but I was looking down the table at Marianne. I was leaning back in my chair, feeling so great looking at Marianne. All of sudden

I mouthed the words to her, "I love you." She looked back at me confused. "What?" she mouthed back.

Later that evening I drove Marianne home. I was driving my brother's car, a van with a big front engine that put an engine cover right between Marianne and me. It was a little awkward and not very romantic.

As I pulled up in front of Marianne's place, I turned to her and said, "You know, I've always said if I ever told a girl I loved her, I would ask her to marry me. Marianne," I continued, "I love you. Would you marry me?"

Marianne was quiet for a few moments. She didn't answer immediately. She was quiet for long enough that I started to get worried.

Finally I asked her, "Well?"

She was in shock that this had all happened so fast. But after a while she turned to me and smiled.

"Yes," she said. "I'll marry you."

That was that. After God threw us together in so many car rides, we made the decision to keep driving together as husband and wife.

Marianne and I kept our engagement a secret for a week or two. We'd come into staff meetings and sit on opposite sides of the table from one another, as if nothing was going on. It was fun to share this big secret just between us. But eventually everybody in Campus Crusade found out, and when they did, the first thing the guys did was to pick me up and put me under a cold shower! Everyone was so excited for Marianne and me and threw us a big party. They had a lot of laughs at our expense. For example, they knew I was into hiking and backpacking while Marianne always looked fashionable and put together. So, as an engagement present, they gave Marianne a big pair of hiking shoes. It was a huge pair of boots – something like a size 14 – the type of thing that a basketball player would wear. Everyone had a big laugh over that.

We were so excited to start out our new life together. After a three-month engagement, Marianne and I married in May of 1968 in Sacramento, California. We didn't have any money to pay for a honeymoon, but two different people loaned us their cabins at Lake Tahoe for a week each. So, we ended up with three-week vacation: one week at one cabin, another week at the next cabin, and a week camping out in a borrowed VW van.

We brought everything we had into our marriage – all our love for God and our hopes for the future. We also brought into marriage our own personalities – our strong wills and past brokenness that we didn't even recognize yet. All that plus a load of camping gear we threw into a car as we headed off on our honeymoon.

God had a lot to teach us!

THE FIRST YEARS
OF MARRIAGE
ALL HAVE SINNED AND FALL SHORT OF THE
GLORY OF GOD (ROMANS 3:23)

Saying our wedding vows wasn't enough to teach us how to be happily married. We both brought our past brokenness into our marriage. We sinned against each other, and we hurt each other as a result.

No human relationships are perfect. The campus ministry we were a part of also experienced trouble. It fractured along political lines, and not long after we were married, we had to find a new church community and a new mission in life.

This chapter in our life story shows just how deep our brokenness goes, and just how much we need God's Holy Spirit.

CHUCK: Something happened on our honeymoon that shows just how messed up we can be, and just how much we need God's help. It was the first week of our honeymoon, and Marianne was making a special dinner for me in the cabin where we were staying. While she prepared dinner, I went out for a walk. Here was beautiful Lake Tahoe! The exaltation of nature! The exhilaration of being married to the woman I love! I hiked around and came back to the cabin grinning from ear to ear. When I opened up the door, there was Marianne, beaming. She gestured to a beautiful cake just out of the oven and cooling on the counter.

Now before I tell about my reaction, I should back up to give you a little bit of background information having to do with Marianne and sweets. When we were in Campus Crusade together, before we got married, Marianne had confided in me that she wanted to lose some weight. Not only that (and this is a terrible idea that we wouldn't recommend to anybody in a relationship today), Marianne asked me if I would help her lose weight. I wanted to help! So, I said yes. Plus, I was good at wagging my finger and saying, "Don't eat this." "You don't need that."

All was going well until one day I walked into the Campus Crusade staff kitchen. There was Marianne, sitting on top of the counter, eating out of a gallon ice cream container. When she saw me, she froze. I turned around and walked straight out. Man, was I angry! Everything I had done to help her! Here she was letting me down!

So, you see, this dynamic was in the back of my mind when I came back from my walk around Lake Tahoe and saw Marianne beaming at a cake on the counter. (Another thing in the back of my mind was that I'm not really a sweets person. Marianne likes sweets, but I like things salty. I'm a chips and pretzels guy, myself. Salt is my thing.) So, when Marianne said, "Chuck, look what I baked! I made this beautiful cake for us!" in that moment all this righteous indignation rose up in me. She didn't bake that cake for me! I don't even like cake! Marianne made this cake because she wanted to eat it all herself! I stomped over to that cake and picked it up in my two hands. I said, "You didn't bake this cake for me! You baked it for yourself!" Then I walked over to the garbage can, opened the lid, and threw that cake straight down into the garbage. Yes, that's what I did. I threw the cake in the garbage.

Marianne was so stunned she couldn't even speak. In fact, I don't think she talked to me at all for the rest of the day, nor the day after that for that matter. Not a good idea, especially on your honeymoon.

In Genesis 3, the serpent whispered some dumb things in the woman's ear. "Did God really say you must not eat the fruit from any of the trees in the garden?" (Genesis 3:1). The serpent who spoke back then in the Garden continues to whisper wrong ideas into the ear of every woman and man. And sometimes we act on them. Like by throwing a cake in the garbage.

Fortunately, God provided a way to cover our mistakes. "The LORD

God made clothing from animal skins for Adam and his wife." (Genesis 3:21). The coverings God gave to Adam and Eve as they left the garden point to what Jesus would later accomplish when He died on the cross. Jesus took the beating that we rightly deserved so that we could be forgiven, freed of our sins, and healed of our brokenness. But first we have to admit our brokenness to him.

In my case it was issues of anger and control that gave the Devil a foothold that afternoon on our honeymoon. There were deeper anger issues with my dad that hadn't been dealt with yet.

After the cake incident, I asked Marianne and God to forgive me for how I hurt her with my words and actions. But in the meantime, I (and Marianne) had to suffer for a long time in brokenness.

The Christian organization we were a part of was suffering from brokenness too. By the time we got married, there had started to be ideological splits within Campus Crusade. Some Campus Crusade directors were saying they didn't want to be an arm of the church. They wanted to be the church. They didn't just want to be on campuses. They wanted to be living in community doing all aspects of the Christian life together. Many people who were at the top of leadership in Campus Crusade left to start something new. By the time we heard about all this, Marianne was pregnant with our first child. It didn't feel right to us to be supported by an organization in chaos.

Many former Campus Crusade staffers were wondering what God was calling us to do next. In this turmoil, I got invited to an event at Big Bear, California. Many ex-crusade leaders and other staff were there to discuss the future. My sister was also on staff by that time and we went together. The former international director of Campus Crusade invited a former Southern Baptist Minister and evangelist who was an author and speaker to address the group.

This speaker addressed the group on the topic of God's Eternal Purpose. He spoke about the power of community. He spoke with a lot of energy. Everything he said was very biblical.

When I heard him speak, it was as if God were speaking to me. After the meeting I got in the car with my sister to leave, and we were struck silent. We couldn't talk for about half an hour afterwards.

After that conference I returned home to Corvallis. When I got home, I said to Marianne, "This is it. We've got to be a part of this." So, we moved to Eugene, Oregon and I got a job teaching elementary school. We formed a house church with ex staff and students of Campus Crusade.

A while later one of the student leaders who had been at the Big Bear conference called a meeting for any students, leaders, and ex-Crusade staff who wanted to come to UCLA to talk and pray about next steps. Many leaders gave formal talks at the gathering. Towards the end of the gathering the same man who spoke so powerfully at Big Bear was invited to speak. He talked more about God's Eternal Purpose and about how we as followers of Jesus can express God as a community.

Out of that meeting at UCLA the student leaders at UCSB in Isla Vista invited that same man to come on a monthly basis to teach them about church life.

Returning to Isla Vista after that gathering, the UCSB group continued to hold spontaneous meetings where people would break into song and tell each other about how they were experiencing God from day to day. They did baptisms in the ocean. They shared everything they had with each other, just like the community of early Christians in the book of Acts.

A group of about 30 of us were doing the same thing in Eugene, Oregon. We visited Isla Vista, and we felt strongly that we should move there to be a part of it all. Our entire group moved together to Isla Vista in 1972 – approximately thirty-four of us.

LIVING IN A CHRISTIAN COMMUNITY
THEY HELD EVERYTHING IN COMMON
(ACTS 4:32)

During the Jesus Movement in the United States in the 1970s, many young people experimented with communal living. In the church community we were a part of in Isla Vista, we were trying to practice first century Christianity, sharing everything in common with one another. This lifestyle had its pros and cons. On the positive side, the spiritual experiences were amazing. We felt God's presence in the meetings and the singing. And we enjoyed sharing life so closely with other believers. We loved living in community and investing ourselves in other people's lives.

But there were negatives, too, especially when it came to our marriage. We didn't have boundaries in place to protect us in our relationship as a couple. Our work for the church took most of our time and attention. Also, as is often the case, the leader of our group exerted an excessive amount of influence. His agenda was more important than anything else, and that often drove us apart in our marriage. So, even as our faith in Jesus grew, our list of hurts grew as well.

MARIANNE: From the beginning, my marriage to Chuck was tied into the work we were doing together for God. For the most part, this was amazing. I loved God, and I loved Chuck. We both loved living in community with other Christians. And we loved the work that we were doing helping people experience God for the first time. But there were consequences to always putting the church first. I would have never said it out loud at the time, but as a new wife I often felt left behind in Chuck's grand spiritual vision. I didn't feel like I came first in his eyes. Something that happened early in our marriage while we were still living in Oregon proved it to me.

On our first wedding anniversary I was seven months pregnant and showing and feeling it. But I was excited to get all dressed up and go to celebrate our first year of marriage together out with my husband to a fancy restaurant. But during dinner Chuck kept checking his watch. It turns out Chuck had to race home after our date, because he had invited three men over to our apartment to listen to a set of cassette tapes. The tapes were of a sermon recording of the charismatic leader Chuck idolized so much. He was talking about the "authentic church." At the time, the split among Campus Crusade staffers was big news, and what to do next was a big deal question. In Chuck's mind these cassette tapes held the answer, and he was determined to share them with some leaders who were traveling in from out of town. Chuck had made this appointment for the Friday night evening of their visit, not remembering that it was our anniversary. He remembered soon enough to take me out to dinner but didn't tell me about his other appointment. So, we had to race out of there to keep the date with the cassettes.

When this sort of thing happened, I didn't know how to feel. If I felt disappointed by Chuck's lack of romance, I also felt ashamed and confused. Chuck was focused on God's work, after all. Did I want to be more important than God's work? If I was mad at Chuck, was I really acting mad at God? Maybe Chuck was more spiritual than I, I worried. Maybe I didn't have enough moral character. Maybe I was falling behind, spiritually speaking.

When we had first met at Campus Crusade, Chuck and I had been on the same spiritual level. We had lots of deep chats over coffee. We were enthusiastic about the work we were doing and about what God would do in the future. But as our lives moved into marriage and then raising young children, our daily preoccupations changed. Chuck was still thinking about his work and about church matters. But I was spending more time caring for children and thinking about the work that needed to get done in our home. When Chuck drove to the conference in Big Bear and heard the amazing speech he wrote about in the previous chapter I wasn't even with him. I was home in Eugene, Oregon. Still, I followed Chuck into what he thought was right. We visited Isla Vista and got involved in that community.

We moved to Isla Vista permanently with thirty-four of our friends when our daughter Amy was two years old and our baby son Andrew was barely three weeks. Right after we moved to Isla Vista, a nasty ideological split occurred within that group. The leader that Chuck admired so much and another leader known in Campus Crusade for Christ had a falling out. They each drew a line in the sand. "You're either with me or you're not." We had moved there with people we had known for several years, and suddenly we were told we couldn't talk to them anymore if they had sided with the other leader. They were our friends and our next-door neighbors! It was horrible.

There were other minor irritations that made me fear that Chuck and I were on separate spiritual levels. Chuck would say, "The other women in the community don't paint their toenails. Why do you have to?" Or he'd say, "The other women don't put artwork on their walls." I liked things to look beautiful. Did this mean I wasn't spiritual enough? When we discussed these things, I felt as if Chuck was on a higher spiritual plane looking down on me. What really upset me was the issue with the dinner plates. We had a lovely set of matching dinnerware that had been given to us as a wedding gift. I loved those plates. Unfortunately for me, the norm of the Isla Vista community had become to share everything in common. This followed a lovely sentiment from the book of Acts: "All the believers were united in heart and mind. And they felt that what they owned was not their own, so they shared everything they had" (Acts 4:32). I don't know how the earliest Christians dealt with dinnerware. But in Isla Vista what it meant was everyone took all the plates and cups and bowls that they had, put them on one big table, and handed them back to people all mixed up. Eventually, the women won out, and we ended up with matching sets, just not our own.

Chuck kept on pushing me to get rid of more. He said that letting go of them should be a spiritual exercise for me. "Why are you holding on to material things?" he asked me. One evening when we were having this fight about holding on to material things, one of the plates went flying across the room. It just missed hitting Chuck in the head as he was running out the door! The plate didn't break. But it did illustrate the challenges we were facing in our new marriage.

Chuck and I wanted to be of one mind with one another, just like when the Bible says, "man leaves his father and mother and is joined to his wife, and the two are united into one" (Genesis 2:24). But we had two different minds going into our marriage. Plus, we faced a spiritual enemy – a force that was set on twisting God's gift of marriage into a mutual torment. "The thief's purpose is to steal and kill and destroy," Jesus said in John 10:10. "My purpose is to give them a rich and satisfying life." Satan found tiny ways to drive Chuck and me apart from the beginning of our lives together. Nothing was safe from the enemy, who the Bible says, "prowls around like a roaring lion" (1 Peter 5:8).

Not even a beautiful act of praise – like raising hands to God – was safe from corruption. Many members of the Isla Vista community liked to throw their hands in the air and say, "Praise the Lord!" when something good happened. They meant it sincerely, but I just couldn't get behind doing it myself. I hadn't grown up around religious people. To me shouting "Praise the Lord" just sounded silly. Chuck teased me about it. In his mind he had this ideal picture of the perfect Christian wife. That wife would be super spiritual and shout "Praise the Lord" like she meant it. One day while we sat on the beach with friends, I let loose with "Praise the Lord!" Chuck got all excited. He pointed to me and said, "You did it!" I felt so embarrassed. My husband was pointing me out in front of everybody. "Humph," I said in my own mind. "You'll never get all of me." In that moment I was just trying to protect myself, but the Bible warns us against making such vows. "But most of all, my brothers and sisters, never take an oath, by heaven or earth or anything else. Just say a simple yes or no, so that you will not sin and be condemned" (James 5:12).

The vow that Chuck would never get all of me came back to haunt me in the coming years. When we were having troubles in our marriage and I wanted to connect with Chuck, I found that I just couldn't do it. Many years later a Christian counselor eventually asked me, "Did you ever make a vow against Chuck?" I realized that I had made a vow on the beach, and that vow was hurting our marriage. I had to choose to forgive Chuck, forgive myself, renounce the vow, and break its power in Jesus' name.

But as I said, all that came much later. In our early marriage, despite the imbalances and disputes, most of the time I loved our family life in Isla Vista. Southern California was an idyllic place to raise young kids. It was 72 degrees almost every day of the year. I took the kids swimming. We went to the beach and dug clams. There were other children to play with, and other stay at home moms to talk to. In those days we had a lot of evening meetings, and everyone would walk from their apartments to the central meeting location where the meeting was held. Early in the evenings you'd see people pour out of their homes onto the street. Someone would say,

"Are you going to the meeting?" and they'd start walking together. More people would come out, and soon it became like a parade. People would link up arm in arm and start singing as we walked down the street. The kids saw this and mimicked it on their own. Our oldest daughter Amy was so much fun to be around. She'd get all the kids marching down the street too. Amy loved to copy whatever the adults were doing. It was so cute to see her marching arm in arm with the other children.

And there were fantastic spiritual experiences in this community, especially for Chuck. At one point the emphasis of the teaching was on being in God's presence all the time. The seventeenth century monk Brother Lawrence had written a book on this, and the leader of our community gave a lot of talks on Brother Lawrence. One day those who could were encouraged to try to do an experiment practicing God's presence. As Chuck and his friend prayed, the presence of God came heavily over Chuck. It was so thick it felt to Chuck like he was sitting in a cloud. This was like nothing Chuck had ever experienced before. He had experienced God before, but this was different. The heavy presence of God stayed on Chuck, even when he got up and moved around. It was even there when he went to the bathroom! It lasted all day long. Chuck never forgot that experience to this day. To him it was evidence that God loves us and just wants to be with us.

Unfortunately, while Chuck was having this amazing spiritual experience, I was feeling left out. Amy and I came looking for Chuck towards the end of the day. "What have you been doing all day long in this apartment?" I asked him, indignantly. It was clear Chuck was experiencing a different reality from what Amy and I were experiencing. I thought, "Well, you have the luxury to go off and do that spiritual stuff. But I'm busy taking care of the kids, doing the daily stuff that needs to get done." Not that I would have chosen to pursue that sort of spiritual experience, even if I had the time. Chuck was the one with the seeker personality. I never wanted to try out new spiritual experiences. Later in life when I did have a powerful experience of the Holy Spirit, I was grateful that God doesn't only come to people who are gung-ho. All I had to do was give God just a little permission eventually. Then it happened for me too.

At the time, the spiritual disconnect between me and Chuck was growing. And it was worst of all when it came to the community's charismatic leader. Chuck was 100% loyal to him. But to me, there were many things this leader did that were off-putting. For example, this leader made belittling comments to some of the women. At one point I confronted him, saying, "I don't think this is right." He responded: "You know what your problem is Marianne? You don't understand, you're married." In other words, I wasn't allowed to have an opinion because I was a married woman. Boy did that tick me off. I felt dismissed.

This man really did not like to be challenged as leader. And when I challenged him, he held a grudge against me. Two years later he got back at me. My parents were visiting, and there was a big meeting in Santa Barbara, in which he publicly humiliated me in front of everyone. "You people are a bunch of bellyachers," he said in front of the whole church. "And Marianne is the biggest bellyacher of them all." I was horrified. Here was my mother who had come to visit. She wasn't a long-time churchgoer herself. When she heard the leader insult her daughter in front of the whole church, she turned bright red. I pulled the leader aside later and told him how upset he had made my mother. He just shot back at me with another pointed comment. "If your mother is anything like my wife's mother," he said, "then she deserved it." I felt dismissed again.

To sum up: beauty and brokenness went hand in hand in both that early Christian community and in my early married relationship with Chuck.

TRAGEDY IN BELGIUM
IF I SETTLE ON THE FAR SIDE OF THE SEA
(PSALM 139:9)

After five years of living in our insular Christian community, we got the chance to strike out on our own as part of the direction the community was going. An opportunity opened up to live and work in Europe. It would mean a change of scenery, a chance to spread the gospel, and time to reconnect as a family. We jumped at the chance.

We had three young children when we packed our bags for Belgium. We were excited to head out on our new adventure. Perhaps we were naïve. We had no idea what was about to happen. Just a few months after moving to Liège, Belgium, everything changed in an instant. We were forced to reevaluate what we believed about God and God's plan for us. And nothing would ever be the same again.

MARIANNE: Our European adventure started with a conference in Isla Vista called "Weltblick." In German this means "worldview." Our leader came up with the idea. Weltblick was to get people excited about going to another country to share the gospel.

Many people in our community were leaving for countries like Germany or Thailand. Those who were trained as teachers were particularly in demand. They could get jobs teaching English in those countries and build Christian community on the side. Chuck was trained as a teacher. I loved all things French, and we wanted to spread the gospel. So Weltblick was right up our alley. Chuck applied for teachings jobs and found one in Belgium in an international school.

Our children were excited to go to Belgium, especially our daughter Amy who had just turned seven. She loved learning French in school, and she was excited to meet new French-speaking playmates. She was a vivacious little kid, always eager to hop up and try something new. Amy's excitement was mimicked by her four-year-old brother Andrew and our daughter Ingrid who was almost two.

We left for Belgium in August, 1976. It was lovely traveling together as a family. We saw all the sights. We experienced European culture and exposed our children to new delights. New foods. Ancient castles. After the background tension of the past few years, it was a relief to be acting like tourists on our own in a foreign land. Amy started a French-speaking school in September, and we settled into our new European lifestyle. Chuck started his teaching job at the international school, and we all started making new friendships and connections.

At the end of the first semester teaching, we decided to take a trip to Norway for Christmas to see some of Chuck's relatives. We were travelling from Liège, Belgium to Norway with close friends from our Isla Vista community who were living and teaching in Germany with their two children. They owned a big Volkswagen van. Back in those days, vans didn't have sliding doors. The doors just opened out if you pushed on them. The van didn't have seatbelts either, and there were no such things as kids car-seats. Our children sat three in a row on the backseat benches, with Christmas gifts piled high behind them. If they looked out the window, they could see a light dusting of snow falling on the road. Christmas magic. As we started the drive, however, we realized that the snow was making it slow going. With the guys taking turns behind the wheel, we had been driving all night and all day from Liège, and the trip was taking longer than expected. With each passing hour, Chuck and I told each other, "Just a little bit further. Just a little bit further."

By the time the sun set, the kids were whining and Chuck and I and our friends were tired.

"It's not worth driving through the night," Chuck said. "I'll pull off at the next exit to find some place to stay." We were in Sweden, near a town called Ängelholm.

I turned around in my seat to encourage the children.

"Okay kids," I said. "We're going to find a place to sleep. If you all be really quiet now, then when we get to the hotel you can each open up one Christmas present." Always obedient, Amy said, "I'll be good" and then sat up stick straight in her seat, zipped her lips, and sat on her hands. As Chuck pulled the car off the exit towards Ängelholm, Sweden, just off the freeway the road made a curve on a downward sloping hill. The van wasn't moving very fast, but the wheels were unstable in the snow. I didn't see it coming. One second I was inside the car, and the next second I was on my bottom in a foot of snow. All the doors of the van had flung open. All our belongings were upended into the snowbank, the Christmas presents, our luggage. I looked around in shock. I was so stunned that I didn't do anything. "God, why did you let this happen?" I thought. I felt nothing but anger.

Four-year-old Andrew was deep in the snow. I tried to get my feet under me. Then I heard Chuck yelling from inside the car. "Come quick! It's Amy." As I approached the car, I saw Chuck leaning over Amy, giving her mouth to mouth resuscitation. Right before the accident Amy had been sitting on the floor behind Chuck. Next to her was a wooden toolbox where our friends had stashed their tools. When the car skidded off the road, Amy was thrown straight ahead into the toolbox. Her temple hit the sharp edge of the box.

An off-duty police officer had seen the car skid off the road. His name was Rune, and he and his wife Birgitta have since become our lifelong friends. Rune was very kind and helpful. He came immediately to the scene of the accident, and he was especially impacted because he had a daughter the exact same age as Amy. He called the paramedics who arrived within minutes. They took Amy in the back of the ambulance, trying to revive her. Chuck and I sat in the front seat. Chuck turned to me and said, "Our life will never be the same after this." We didn't say much else the rest of that day. We sat outside the hospital operating room and waited and waited. After a long time, a doctor came out and told us, "Amy is dead." We didn't respond. We heard the doctor, but it was as if we hadn't heard the doctor. All I remember thinking was, "Where was God?" "Where were you, God, when the accident happened?" How could a perfect child be here one minute and gone the next minute? Had God turned his head? Why did He let the accident happen?

Nobody knew what to do with a grieving family. People said things to me like, "It was part of God's plan. If Amy had been living in a house in

Santa Barbara, she could have fallen out of a tree and died." That didn't make sense to me. God doesn't give you a beautiful kid so He can snatch her back again.

Before Amy's death, Chuck and I had thought that once you gave your life to Jesus everything would be good. That's what we imagined when we got married. That's the picture we had in our minds when we moved to Belgium to spread the gospel in French. But that's not what Jesus said. He never said life would be easy. Jesus warned his disciples that they would face pain and loss. "Here on earth you will have many trials and sorrows" (John 16:33). A safe and easy life wasn't the reality for Jesus. And it wasn't the reality for Jesus' first disciples either. Most of them died young of terrible deaths. Jesus knew that the world was a risky place.

The world is risky because people have free will. God could have made us all robots who love Him, but He gave us choice. And so, everywhere, all over the world, people are making choices that may or may not be wise, safe, or godly. We chose to drive at night when we were tired, for example. Our friends chose to put a toolbox between the front two seats of their van. Everyone's choices add up to a world that is full of risk. But even as Jesus warned his disciples of this, he offered them hope. "Here on earth you will have many trials and sorrows. But take heart, because I have overcome the world" (John 16:33).

The Bible goes on to say that our present trials – from the horrible deaths the disciples faced to the horror of losing a child – all these sorrows are nothing compared to the good things that God has in store for us. "Our present troubles are small and won't last very long. Yet they produce for us a glory that vastly outweighs them and will last forever!" (2 Corinthians 4:17). What a bold claim. In comparison to God's glory – which we'll get to see some day – our present troubles are small and temporary. How can this even be possible? My beautiful child was here one minute, and the next minute she was gone. How could any goodness make that pale in comparison? How could anything possibly be that good? It's hard to imagine. But after Amy's death I got several tiny glimpses of this glory that God says will make it feel okay.

The summer after Amy died, two of our friends went up to Ängelholm, Sweden to create a photo album for us. They took pictures of Amy's grave site and walked around the beautiful city. At the front of the album, my friend pasted an image of the town's crest: a child with wings looking over two fishes and a crown. She explained the history of Ängelholm: the "hospitality corner of Sweden." Next to pictures of lush green parks and quaint European cottages, she copied Bible verses in her neat handwriting. "I will not leave you – I will come to you" (John 14:18). The last two photos in the album show the grass growing over Amy's grave, and the crossroads entering the city. Then there is a gap of two white pages. Starting on the next page, my friend imagined Amy's new life in heaven. She pasted storybook illustrations of children playing next to words she'd written out as if in Amy's hand:

> *Heaven is really neat!! I mean you wouldn't believe how many friends are here. Yes, I suppose there are times I miss earth… but it's because we know parents miss us.*

> *Time passes so quickly – remember how you always reminded me to pick up? Well – guess what – somehow I don't mind it here. I don't know why that's different??*

> *I just love the kids – we play all kinds of games. I still take gymnastics. I have a super teacher!*

> *Jesus loves for us to put on plays for him. So we dress up and dance. Oh, Dad and Mom, Jesus is so neat – I'm so glad you told me about him – WOW!! He helps me with my flips and cartwheels.*

> *Paul helps us "write." It's special kind of writing – hard to explain --- something like – when I "write" and tell you special love messages Jesus puts them in your heart – we don't even have to mail them like on earth. – hard to explain…*

> *We have lots of parties – Jesus told us about a wedding party he was at once long ago. But he said our parties are neater!*

> *Everything is wonderful – and time goes so fast – it's all different here. You will see someday. Jesus promised we can have a party when you come – it will be so-o-o neat!!*

> *I love you.*

These words and pictures gave me comfort when I couldn't hear comfort from my own prayers.

Decades later, at a Holy Spirit conference in Toronto, I got a confirmation of the truth that my friend had written down in this album. A woman got up to speak about an experience she'd had during worship time.

She'd seen a glimpse of heaven: everybody was singing and dancing just like in a worship service. God showed her all the kids in heaven – the children who had died before their time. They were dancing and having a great time. The name of that conference was "The Party is Here." At that moment it hit me. It was true what God spoke to me through that album. *Jesus promised we can have a party when you come.*

God also sent me a message through my mother shortly after Amy's death. My mom didn't go to church. She wasn't against God – she just didn't talk about Him very much. But when she came to Liège to help us after Amy's death, my mom brought a message for me that she had written on a thin piece of onion skin paper. "I don't know whether I had a vision or a dream," she told me "But I woke up in the middle of the night and I knew I had to write this down." What she wrote down on that thin paper was a conversation titled "Amy and the Lord."

> *"Come, Amy," said the Lord.*

> *"Oh, where am I? It sure is nice here. Really pretty. But I must go my mommy and daddy will miss me."*

> *"It is all right, Amy. I am Jesus."*

> *"Oh, my mommy and daddy know you and talk and sing about you all the time. So I guess they won't mind if I stay awhile. It sure is pretty here!"*

That thin piece of paper from my mother meant so much to me.

If I'd awakened having dreamt that conversation between God and Amy myself, I would have thought it was just wishful thinking. "I'm just dreaming. That isn't real," I would have told myself. I would never have believed God if He'd given the message to me directly. But because God gave it to my mom, because that was so unlike her, I believed. And that brought me a lot of comfort.

PROBLEMS IN OUR MARRIAGE

SEE THAT NO ROOT OF BITTERNESS SPRINGS UP AND CAUSES TROUBLE (HEBREWS 12:15)

Unprocessed grief took its toll on us. We kept a brave face as we moved back from Belgium to the United States with two young children. We reacclimated to life in the United States. But the problems we'd never addressed stayed simmering beneath the surface. Issues of control and unforgiveness separated us from one another. When we moved back into a close-knit church community, all hell broke loose in our marriage. A huge breach of trust led us into marriage counseling. We started to look at our past. And we realized just how much we needed God to bring us to wholeness.

CHUCK: I couldn't really process my feelings of grief after Amy's death. I shut my emotions off. I had to be a spiritual leader, both for my family and for my extended community. To me, that meant I couldn't just be a hurting person, desperate for God. Marianne cried herself to sleep for over a year. For her sake I thought I had to stay "strong." I had to stay in control.

To prove to everyone that I was doing okay, that I was strong, I made a cassette tape in Belgium and sent it to our friends back home. On the tape I talked about Amy's death in detached spiritual terms. I expressed assurance that Amy was in heaven. I praised God for His sovereignty. I even quoted some Bible verses. I conveyed the image that I was completely accepting, completely in control. But inside I was just numb. I went back to my job teaching school in Liège after one week of extra vacation. Not one person at work said a single thing to me about my loss. Everyone knew that I had lost a daughter over Christmas vacation, but nobody knew what to say to me. So they just didn't say anything. Grief wasn't a topic people talked about. Nobody knew how to deal with us.

Three months after the accident, Marianne and I got a letter from someone in the community in Isla Vista. *I know this time has been hard on you,* the letter basically said. *But it's been three months now. Hearts should be beginning to heal.*

The letter was written in good faith, but the reality is you never get over losing a child.

We did as best we could under the circumstances. We clung together as a family. My parents came to stay with us for a time in Belgium, as did Marianne's parents. We took care of Andrew and Ingrid. We traveled and showed our kids around Europe. And we continued to do the church work we had come to Belgium to do. We lived in a big house filled with Christian community. We kept running conferences and sharing Jesus with people. We soldiered on with our work in Belgium for five and a half years. In some ways it was the perfect place for us to be. We were hidden away, out of church politics, supporting each other as a family. But we couldn't stay in Belgium forever. Andrew was nine years old, played soccer, and dressed like Belgian kids. Ingrid was five and beginning to speak with an accent. If we wanted them to have any American experience, we would have to make our way back to the States. And that meant figuring out what to do next.

The church in Isla Vista was in transition. The community in Santa Barbara had been disbanded by the leader. He was encouraging those of us who wanted to continue working with him to move to Portland, Maine. I had an interview for a teaching job in Maine, but it fell through. So, we decided to move to West Palm Beach. I had a Christian friend in Florida who laid tile for a living. He agreed to show me the ropes of the business. So off we moved to Florida.

It was a happy year in the refuge of Florida. The manual labor made me feel good physically. This year also marked a turning point in Marianne's career. Both children were in school now, and we were low on money. So, I said to Marianne, "You need to get a job." Marianne hadn't thought of going back to work after having children. She didn't know what to do exactly. She started her job search by going to all the schools in the area to see if any of them needed a French teacher. They didn't have any openings for French teachers at the time, but Marianne got a job teaching English as second language to Haitians.

Getting out of the house and working made Marianne feel a whole lot better. She enjoyed having a life outside of me and the kids. Teaching turned out to be tremendously fulfilling for her. In Florida and a year later when we moved to Maine, Marianne earned her license to teach high school, and then another license to teach kindergarten through elementary. In the end, Marianne worked in the public schools for over 20 years.

Marianne refers to our time in Belgium and then in Florida as our "bubble" years. We were on our own, out of church politics, clinging to each other as we raised our two remaining children. It was only after we moved back into our dysfunctional church community that the problems in our marriage really started to surface.

Our charismatic leader had relocated from Isla Vista, California to Portland, Maine. After a year laying tile, I wanted to move closer to be near him. We moved our family to Maine, and in no time at all I was the leader's right-hand man. It was just like before we left for Belgium. Once again, I was consumed with church work for a group of about two dozen people. "Oh no," Marianne thought. "We're back at this again." The old patterns in our marriage emerged in no time.

I put my work for the church ahead of Marianne. She was passive aggressive toward me as a result. I pressured Marianne into being more spiritual. She got angry. All the old issues that we hadn't dealt with since I threw the cake in the garbage and Marianne made that vow on the beach came roaring back. One day while I was out, a friend of mine came by the house looking for me. "Where's Chuck?" the friend asked Marianne. She was at the stove stirring a pot of food, and her anger boiled over. "He's not here, of course!" She snapped. "He's out somewhere doing something for *him*." She was figuratively stewing while literally stewing. I couldn't see at the time what this was doing to our marriage.

Because I was loyal and the leader's right-hand man, I handled the group's money, among other things. Since our "house church" was pretty informal and was never formally incorporated, there were no bylaws, rules, or directives on how to handle money and property.

At the beginning I had been young, naïve, and excited about the Jesus revival of the 1970s. But now I was growing older. I was in my 40s and I was getting help from a respected Christian counselor. I was learning how to have good boundaries and how to share my thoughts and feelings about things. As I grew more mature and started to get freer, the influence of the group's leader on me was changing. A trained counselor even came to mediate between us, which exposed me to my own brokenness but also gave me insight into things I really needed to hear.

The group itself was also evolving. Notably we finally reached a point when four of the younger men and I were officially added to the leadership group alongside of the older leader.

I came to a place where I was no longer comfortable with the way our group handled money, even for a fluid, spontaneous house church. I shared this with the other younger leaders when the older leader was out of town. Our goal was to figure out how to move ahead with new processes, but he saw it differently. Offended that we would question him at all, he left and moved away. It was over. A few of the youngest people went with him. Others went to the four winds. This was hard in many ways, especially for our kids since they were friends with those who left. Our son Andrew was in high school at the time, and he looked up to the single men in the community in their twenties. They would hang around and talk to Andrew after meetings, and those relationships were an encouragement to Andrew. After the leader left, in a flash they were all gone. Our daughter Ingrid can hardly talk about this time without crying, even today. There were kids she babysat – families she loved who moved away suddenly. With our network in tatters, I was now free to turn my attention back to Marianne. It was then that I got a rude awakening.

For the ten years that we had been living in Maine, I had gone to the group leader for all my validation and emotional support. When it came to my relationship with Marianne, I had either neglected her or tried to micromanage her spiritually. From Marianne's point of view, there was very little good she could see in our marriage. When we'd fight, she'd think, "It was a mistake that we ever got married." She started to pull herself farther and farther away from me. She developed her own network of friends. She worked on her teaching credentials. Even living in the same house, she lived a life apart from me, although I couldn't see it. The more we disagreed with one another, the more Marianne thought, "Forget it. This just isn't working. I'm tired of this." And this wasn't only going on in her head. She started acting on these feelings too.

Nobody wakes up one day and decides, "I think I'll have an affair." That's not the way it happens. What happens instead is that people are unhappy, or they're angry. They get attention from somebody new that they're not getting at home. And things progress from there. What happened with Marianne was she became attracted to a man where she worked. When she saw this guy at work, he winked at her. That felt good in a surprising way. Another time she saw him, and she noticed that he was watching her. They held each other's glance a little too long. It felt good to get a little eye contact, a little smile, and the sense that someone might be interested in you.

The first time they kissed, Marianne came home and told me about it. It was at a work Christmas party. Marianne hadn't gone to the party with this guy, but when they left the party, they were alone together in the driveway. I was in bed and almost asleep when Marianne woke me up to tell me she'd kissed this guy. She said it in a very matter-of fact way. "I kissed someone." I don't remember what I said. But I do remember that I got out of bed and walked the streets for several hours. I was furious. I was beside myself. "What is going on?" I kept repeating to myself over and over. What was going on? How could I fix it?

I should pause here to describe something I've taught to hundreds of people in my pastoring work in the time since. I could have used a better understanding of it that night. It's the concept of forgiveness. As much as other people's actions hurt me, unforgiveness hurts me more. If I don't forgive someone else, I'm going to be stuck in my own bitterness and anger. It becomes a sticking point in my relationship with God. Jesus said as much. "When you are praying," Jesus said, "first forgive anyone you are holding a grudge against, so that your Father in heaven will forgive your sins, too" (Mark 11:25). Forgiveness isn't easy. It's a choice. It's something I choose to do to allow God back into my life when I've gotten bent out of shape. These days, when someone hurts me, I pray something like this:

> "I choose to forgive [person's name] for [specific way they hurt me.] I give this person the gift of unconditional forgiveness, and I entrust them to you, God. I bless this person in your name."

Often when I do this, I realize I had an ungodly response to the hurt I experienced. I got angry or judgmental. In addition to forgiving the other person, I have to repent of my ungodly response and ask God to forgive me, too. "God," I'll say, "forgive me for my ungodly response to the hurt I felt. Forgive me for my judgment, bitterness, and anger."

Of course, Marianne wasn't the only one who needed forgiveness at that point in our marriage. I never cheated, but I had been emotionally unfaithful. There was a young woman at the school where I was working. She and I just hit it off. I didn't think anything of it at the beginning. But I liked her so much that when a bunch of my colleagues and I were going on a school field trip, I approached the organizer of the trip to say, "I want to be in the same vehicle with her." That's how obsessed I was with this woman. It turned out that this woman was in fact interested in me, so in her mind my attentions spelled the possibility of "something more." A misunderstanding at a work Christmas party made things even more awkward. Marianne and the young woman were in the bathroom together, when the young woman started gushing about me. "Chuck is your husband?" she said to Marianne. "You're so lucky! He's such a great guy!" Marianne bristled. "If you want him so badly, you can have him!" She said it sarcastically, but little did she know. The woman thought it was great news! She suggested that Marianne and I drive with her and her husband to the after-party. We said okay, and the girl climbed into the front seat next to me, while her husband got in the backseat with Marianne. It was a very awkward drive. Again, our bitterness towards one another had gotten us into a situation where we found ourselves asking, "What is going on?"

I told my men's small group about the awkward situation, and about how much time I was spending with this woman. Since I was open with her about my relationship with Jesus, I rationalized what I was doing! My close friend said, "Chuck, you would never have an affair, but you're having an emotional affair." Those words really hit me. I was having an emotional affair. I was doing something that wasn't right. It just felt so good to have someone listen to me. The next time I saw the woman, I knew I had to break it off. "I can't do this anymore," I told her. "If I'd said to you, 'Let's go get a motel room,' would you have gone?" "Of course!" she said. I was shocked. I had been rather naive. And it hit me hard that my marriage was really in trouble. *I decided Marianne and I had to see a marriage counselor.*

When I suggested it to Marianne, I didn't hide the fact that I thought she was the one who needed more fixing. In fact, I explained this to the counselor when we were together in his office. Our marriage needed fixing because Marianne was acting out. The counselor interrupted me mid-explanation. "Let me just ask you a question," he said. "Marianne, do you feel cherished by this man?" Marianne shot me a pitying look. She didn't say anything. He repeated the question, "Do you feel cherished by Chuck?" "Oh Chuck," she said, patting me on the hand. She didn't want to hurt my feelings. But she really couldn't say that she felt cherished in our marriage. That was a wake-up call for me.

After the counselor talked to both of us, he met with me man-to-man. And he really let me have it. "Chuck, you've got some work to do," he told me. "On you." At his prompting, I started pursuing healing for my own sake. I signed up for a week-long training course with a Christian counselor who specialized in teaching laymen how to counsel.

The counselor leading the course would work with a test-subject every day for the week while all the other students watched on closed-circuit TV. The others got one-on-one counseling privately. Luckily for me, I got picked to be the test subject. That meant intense counseling day after day for a week. We were delving into my past: my feelings about God and my relationship with my father. On the third day of the training, I said, "I need to tell you something." I don't know why, but I felt like I needed to share about the accident – about what happened with Amy. I started telling him about that night in Ängelholm, and suddenly it hit me – all the grief I had been keeping inside for 15 years. All that pent-up emotion burst to the surface. And I started crying. It wasn't just crying. It was a deep physical sobbing that took over my entire body. It went on for two hours. I couldn't stop it. It was long overdue. After the counseling session all the students were supposed to meet together in a room to debrief. I started to walk into that room, and the counselor said, "Chuck, get out of here. You need to go for a walk."

The next day, I came back to counseling with a different feeling. I was hit with the feeling of responsibility. I needed to take ownership over what happened in the accident. I had been driving in unsafe conditions. I needed to recognize my poor choices and ask God's forgiveness. Something I learned about forgiveness that day is that only after I acknowledge my part can I fully receive and enjoy the peace of God's forgiveness. You see, forgiveness isn't only between me and other people. Sometimes the person I need to forgive is myself. It begins with admitting I've done something wrong, then praying something like this:

> "Thank you, God for the cross and for forgiving me all my sin. I choose now to forgive myself for [specific wrongs]. I will no longer hold these things over my life but free myself from them. In Jesus' name."

When something terrible happens, we tend to cast blame in all directions. We blame someone else, we blame ourselves, and we blame God for letting it happen. Getting free means forgiving the people who've harmed us, forgiving ourselves, and finally forgiving God.

Experiencing this new freedom made me think, "Wow. There really is something to this inner healing." It made me even hungrier to go after spiritual healing in my marriage. Marianne and I started seeing a new therapist in Portland, Maine. Sometimes we went together, and sometimes we saw her individually. We were really trying to fix things between us, but the wall of resentment just didn't feel like it was budging. I was doing all the things Marianne said might make her happy. I was bringing her flowers and taking her on dates. But Marianne's demeanor towards me didn't change. She just wasn't feeling the good feelings that I had hoped for from my nice gestures. Marianne didn't understand why she couldn't find love for me anymore. She even wondered to herself, "Chuck is trying so hard. He's buying me flowers. Why don't I like it?" The answer would start to come clear in an individual session with our therapist.

One day, in one of her individual sessions with Marianne, the therapist asked a question that finally set the healing in motion. "Do you think you ever made a vow against Chuck?" she asked Marianne. A vow? Marianne had never heard the word used in those terms before. She knew about marriage vows, but not about vows you make against a person you love. Suddenly, she remembered that day on the beach where she said silently, "You'll never get all of me." Could that be a vow? Marianne thought about it for a while. It seemed that, yes, those words she spoke on the beach were affecting our marriage still.

The counselor invited Marianne to break the vow. But Marianne wasn't so sure she wanted to. After all, those words were protecting her from my judgement. How would Marianne feel if she weren't holding anything back anymore? How could she be emotionally safe from me? As Marianne thought through the issue, a close friend gave her some gentle advice. "It's your choice, Marianne," her friend said. "You don't need to do anything. You can keep your vow if you want, or you can break it. If you don't do anything, probably nothing will change in your marriage. But if you do renounce the vow, you might see something happen. You never know. It's up to you." This encouragement to choose for herself gave Marianne the freedom she needed. Marianne chose to break the vow in the presence of the counselor.

In that next session, Marianne first forgave me for my past hurtful behavior that had prompted her to make a vow against me. The hurt I had caused her needed to be released. Then she forgave herself for making the vow that had contributed to the wasting of years of emotional separation. And lastly, she released all the power the vow was holding over her. She said something like this:

> "I renounce the vow of [you'll never have all of me]. By the power and authority of Jesus, I break this vow. I release my spirit soul and body to no longer feel, think and act according to this vow."

The counselor prayed that Marianne would be restored to her original design and to be able to appreciate the good things in our marriage. After Marianne broke that vow, I noticed a significant change in our relationship. We started connecting more. When I brought her flowers, she appreciated it. We started liking each other more. Still, we were far from completely healed. As we were going to counseling and working through these issues, something happened to us financially that showed me just how much I need Jesus's forgiveness.

At my teaching job I had been contributing to a 403(b) investment account. The school would take out the money every month, and that had been going on for years. I had accumulated a lot of money, and I was a little bit obsessed with that money. If I had a break in my school day, I'd log into my account to see the balance and how much it was earning (or losing). I didn't think of this as an ungodly obsession. I told myself it was all for God. "I want to retire and work for God," I'd say to myself. "So, this money is important. It's important to manage it and keep it growing." As a faithful Christian, I had a financial accountability partner who went through all my investments to make sure they were on the up-and-up. Still, I wanted to push the envelope. I wanted the money to grow faster.

I met a man at a Christian conference who made investments and had made some good profits with his money. He encouraged me to go to an investment conference with the hopes of making even more money. At the conference, in one of the side rooms, I got pitched an investment vehicle which sounded too crazy not to try. This was in the days of the dot com bubble, and all investments were making money. The big question was not just how to make money, but how to make the most money out of your investments. The guy who made the pitch was quite convincing. The accounts would just go up and up. I thought, "Gee, if I invest it all with him this way, I'll make more money and be able to retire sooner. Then I can do more for God!" I didn't tell my financial accountability partner. I didn't tell Marianne. I knew they would try to talk me out of it. And I was determined to write a check for the entire amount in our savings. After all, it was for God.

Soon after I had given this guy all the money in that school retirement account, I could tell something was off. I didn't think he was dishonest, but he hadn't set up the fund properly and had invested everything in one stock. Meanwhile, the dot com bubble started to burst. The fund manager and I had a series of very shaky phone calls. On the last of these terrible calls, I learned that the fund manager was going to jail. All of our money was gone. All of it. I remember I dropped to my knees on the living room floor and cried. "It's gone, it's all gone!" What had I done? The next terrible thought was that I had to tell Marianne. She was in shock. She had trusted me completely to manage our money. Marianne forgave me, but her trust in me was broken once again.

We were even more desperate than before and we needed God to help us.

RENEWAL IN TORONTO
I WILL POUR OUT MY SPIRIT ON ALL FLESH
(JOEL 2:28)

God had more healing in store for us. But we had to take a risk and leave the comfort of our past church experience behind. We were very cautious about anyone who talked too much about the Holy Spirit. In those days in Campus Crusade you had to leave if you spoke in tongues. We knew people affiliated with the charismatic renewal of the 1960s and 1970s. It had all seemed strange. And yet, there was still a part of us that was open to learning more. In the 1990s we had heard about a revival going on at a church in Canada that featured some extreme manifestations of the Holy Spirit that were outside anything we'd ever seen before. At first, we were both skeptical. It took several leaps of faith to get us out of our comfort zones. But when we opened ourselves up just a little bit to the Holy Spirit, miracles started to happen. We felt God's love for us in a new way. We suddenly felt connected to each other. And we realized that God had more for us.

CHUCK: Our son Andrew was the first one to tell us about his own experience of being touched by the Holy Spirit. Starting when he was in high school, Andrew had done lots of reading about Christian counseling and inner healing. He was trying to heal from the residual effects of his sister's death, and he was a pretty serious kid. When he went away to college at Stanford, Andrew got involved with Intervarsity Christian Fellowship and traveled to many of their events. At one retreat, while he was getting prayed for, Andrew had this wild experience of the Holy Spirit. Andrew fell on the ground giggling, laughing, and rolling on the floor. It left a lasting impact on him. His friends even nicknamed him "Happy Andy," which was funny because Andrew was typically so serious. This was the first story Marianne and I heard where a validated encounter with the Holy Spirit left a lasting effect on the person.

Meanwhile, a church in Toronto, Canada was seeing new openings for miraculous healings, both physical and emotional. Burned out believers were getting excited about God again. Like other revivals throughout history, the things going on at this church were exuberant signs of God's love. People were falling down on the floor, laughing uncontrollably, or making odd noises. These funny signs pointed to deeper things happening in people's lives as a result of visiting this church. Folks reported incurable diseases being healed, or difficult relationships getting turned around – all because they had made a trip to Toronto and fallen down on the floor under the influence of the Holy Spirit.

I was initially skeptical of what I heard about this movement. But there were several signs that I needed to check it out for myself. The first was a conversation I had with some guests from Switzerland. These young guys stopped by at our house in Maine on their way to Toronto. They told me they were going to Toronto to witness what the Holy Spirit was doing. At that I got a little sarcastic. "Oooh," I teased, thinking about all the weird reports I had heard. "You're going to see the Holy Spirit? When you peel yourself off the ground you'll have to tell me all about it." On their trip back from Toronto we met again in my living room. Again, I asked sarcastically, "How was your visit with the Holy Spirit?" This young guy turned to me and pulled me up short. "Chuck, you better be careful how you speak about the Holy Spirit," he said. I felt reprimanded, but in a convicting sort of way. God was trying to tell me something. The Holy Spirit is not a joke. It's time to take Him seriously.

Another witness to the Toronto renewal was a friend I had known in Norway. He had been in Toronto for business when he went to some meetings at the church. "I was on the floor for three days," he reported to me. "All I did was cry." This didn't sound very good to me – crying on the floor for three days? But the guy acted as if it was the best thing that had ever happened to him. "You should check it out," he said.

Suddenly it seemed like everyone was talking to me about Toronto. A friend in another city described a local service where the pastor from Toronto had visited. So many people fell down while getting prayed for that my friend had to serve as a "catcher" – a designated volunteer who was assigned to catch people before they hit the floor. My friend told me, "The person praying doesn't even touch them. It's not like they're getting pushed. He might just touch them gently on the hand, and the person falls over." He ended by saying, "You should really check it out. There's definitely something going on."

The last sign that I should go to Toronto was a really crazy coincidence. Marianne and I were on vacation in Washington state. While taking a boat ride from Anacortes to the San Juan Islands, suddenly I said, "That guy over there – I think he is a pastor that I met at a conference last year." I went over to say hello, and he said to me, "Guess what? We just came from a conference in Toronto. We were up there for nine days, and it was amazing. You have to go there." I asked the pastor on the boat to tell me more. "What you have to do," he instructed me, "is wait until the end of the meeting. When they ask people to come forward for prayer, that's your cue. Get right up there to the front. There's more power in the front." I thought that sounded a bit weird. But in my head, I was taking notes. I really wanted this experience. "God is going to come over you," he continued. "But whenever you can stand again, get up and get more prayer." He ended by saying, "Stay as long as you can." When I got off that boat ride, I had my marching orders and now I was convinced God was trying to tell me something. I was ready go to Toronto and experience this wild kind of prayer. Marianne, however, was not so interested.

Marianne did not want to go. She wasn't interested in trying something new – especially another new spiritual thing into which I was trying to push her. She said, "You can do whatever you want, but I'm not going." In our marriage counseling, she was just beginning to set better boundaries. So now when I wanted her to come to Toronto, Marianne said, "I don't have to do everything you're doing." So, I made plans to go with a friend instead.

Marianne and I had a week-long stint visiting a Young Life camp at Lake Saranac New York. At the end of the week, my friend and I were supposed to drive from the camp to Toronto. Marianne arranged her own transportation back to Portland. But at the last minute, my friend backed out and changed his plans. "Please," I pleaded with Marianne. "We're halfway there. I don't want to drive all by myself and stay in an empty hotel." She shook her head, No. "Come on," I continued. "You don't have to go to the church meetings. You can just take the credit card and go shopping." Eventually Marianne relented. With great excitement in my heart, we drove up to Toronto together.

Marianne and I were nervous going into our first meeting. We felt out of place in the midst of a revival. In the room of about 3,000, Marianne and I sat in the last row in the last two chairs. We wanted to be able to make an exit just in case things got too weird. And let me tell you, things got weird. Somebody would be talking up front, giving a biblical message, and there would be sections of the audience that suddenly started laughing. Like 500 people on the left-hand side of the room would all start laughing at the same time. The message wasn't funny, but all these people would start laughing like they weren't even listening. Then they would do a worship song, and people would be shaking. They were shaking so fast that you'd think they would get whiplash. Or they'd jump up and down. But many more just lay still in God's presence. There were all kinds of strange things. The talks were good and biblical. The thing that impressed Marianne most of all was that they had a lot of visitors. People who had never had a relationship with Jesus before were coming to the meetings. At the end of each service, the pastor would give an invitation to come forward if you wanted to meet Jesus. Hordes of people would go streaming down the aisles. For someone who had spent a lifetime working in evangelism, that was pretty exciting. Still, she wasn't comfortable with all the odd behavior in the church service, and as soon as the official meeting ended Marianne bolted for the door. But I didn't leave with her. I had my instructions to go to the front of the room to get prayer.

While Marianne hurried back to the hotel room, I walked forward. There were lots of people praying and getting prayer at the front of the church. I was a bit nervous, but a nice old guy with white hair approached me. He asked if he could pray for me, and I was relieved to say yes. He just started praying for me to receive the Holy Spirit. Suddenly, I felt peace. I had never felt anything like that before. The Holy Spirit came over me, and I crumpled right there on the floor. I was totally conscious, but I didn't want to get up. When I got back to the hotel room, Marianne asked how it was. "I feel like I just had a warm bath in God," I told her. "A warm bath in God?" Marianne thought. "That is the weirdest thing I've ever heard." And just like that, we were back to our old dynamic. I had experienced something spiritual that Marianne hadn't. And now she was mad at me.

MARIANNE: For the next three days I was miserable in Toronto. I went to meetings with Chuck, but I would leave at the end when it came time for prayer. I was mad that he had dragged me into yet another crazy spiritual adventure. Here he was, launching headlong into some new type of wild church experience, and I was just expected to tag along as always. I was really annoyed. At one point as we sat outside the hotel in our car, Chuck broke down crying. "I'm sorry I brought you up here." He said to me. "I'm sorry I talked you into this." Seeing him feel so terrible, my heart opened up to Chuck little bit. After all, there were good things happening in those Toronto meetings, even if I didn't like the style. People were becoming believers. The stories from the front of the church were amazing. People would share during the church service things like: "Last night I got prayer, and I forgave my dad." Or couples would talk about reuniting after years of estrangement. I knew that it couldn't be all bad. Seeing Chuck break down in the car, I lowered my defenses. I said in my heart, "Okay God. If this is from you, then I want to know." That's all the permission that God needed. He never overrides my free will, but he often jumps in if I give him just a little bit of permission.

The next morning Chuck and I went to the meeting, and I took my walking shoes. My plan was to get some exercise after the meeting and come back to collect Chuck for lunch. When I finished my walk most of the church was empty. Chuck was somewhere near the front, and I had to walk through all the rows of empty chairs to find him. As I slowly neared the front of the building, I remember thinking, "Man, I'm really getting close to the front of this thing." Chuck saw me approaching, and he ran up excitedly. "Do you want to get prayer?" he asked for the millionth time. "No, no, no," I said. "What if you don't have to ask someone?" he tried again. "What if I go get somebody and bring them here?" "Well," I hesitated for just a moment. That was all the little window Chuck needed. "I'll be right back," Chuck said. He was off and running.

Chuck came back with this little woman to pray for me. She was petite, with long blonde hair tied up in a gold clip. She was wearing nice gold jewelry and a stylish silk top. On top of that, she had a French accent, and I was absolutely nuts for everything French. I thought, "Oh, she doesn't look too religious. I guess I'll let her pray." She asked me if she could pray for me, and I said, "Okay."

"Do you ever raise your hands to praise the Lord?" she asked.

"Oh no," I said, "I could never do that. I'm just way too uptight."

"Oh." She said. "Well, can you just put out your hands like you're going to receive a present?"

"I guess I can do that," I said. The woman said, "You don't need to pray or do anything. I'll pray. You just receive." That really took the pressure off

44

me. She started to pray for the Holy Spirit, and immediately my knees felt like Jello. I couldn't hold myself up anymore. I fell backwards, and Chuck caught me. Carefully, he laid me down on the floor.

The minute my head touched the floor I heard a voice in my head. "All I want to do is love you," God said to me. It was different from anything I had ever heard before, but I knew the voice was from God.

"Is that all this is about?" I wondered. "God just wants to love me?" I was startled by how simple that message was. "This is what I've been fighting for three days? That God just wants to love me?" I lay there on the floor for a few minutes. Then I started giggling. Chuck got someone to pray for him too, and before long we were both lying on the ground, giggling like two little kids. It was kind of cool.

We went back to our hotel room that evening, and as we were going up the elevator, we just looked at each other. Again, we started giggling. Two grown-ups giggling in an elevator – it doesn't sound like much of anything on the outside. But to us, it was a miracle. We had been through so much pain and hurt and anger. We didn't know whether our marriage was going to survive. And then suddenly God came over us with this new experience of the Holy Spirit. And the biggest thing God had to tell us? "Quit taking yourselves so seriously. Just enjoy the moment." We couldn't stop giggling and looking at one another. Finally, we were experiencing God together, equally, and at the same time.

After I gave the Holy Spirit permission, He gave me more exciting supernatural experiences. Chuck and I went back again for prayer that night, and the same French woman prayed for me. Again, I fell down and had a deep experience of God's love. The next morning, I practically ran to the front of the room for prayer. The French woman wasn't there that day, so a different lady offered to pray for me. I had a momentary doubt: "Is this going to work? Will it happen if it's not the same lady?" But it turned out to work no matter who was praying. The power was coming from the Holy Spirit. After getting prayer I lay on the floor thinking, "Oh thank you, God. This is so peaceful." As I said this, my left arm started moving, kind of quickly. I thought, "Wait, my arm is moving, but I'm not moving my arm." Then the other arm started moving. They were moving so fast it was as if they were motorized. I thought to myself, "This is weird. I don't believe in this kind of stuff." When I had first come to the meetings and seen people shaking, I'd said, "I don't ever want to do that. Don't let that happen to me!" But just the night before, a pastor from England had given a talk that really changed my thinking on this. He explained, "Whenever an outpouring of the Holy Spirit happens, we need to ask ourselves: 'What does it mean and what is it for?'" In his opinion, the point of the renewal in Toronto was to touch everyone that knew Jesus and get their hearts back to the love of God.

There's a passage at the beginning of the book of Revelation, where Jesus rebukes church leaders who have lost their passion. Jesus says, "But I have this complaint against you. You don't love me or each other as you did at first!" (Revelation 2:4). I was one of those people who knew Jesus, but who had lost my excitement over the years. Tragedy and bitterness had sapped it from me. It was also true in my marriage with Chuck. I had lost my first love. Even though the manifestations seemed unusual, the laughing and the shaking each had their purpose. So, when I found myself on the ground with my hands moving like a motor, I asked God the same question the speaker from the previous evening posed to us, "What does this mean and what is it for?" I heard in my head, "Marianne, I'm going to loosen you up so you can raise your hands to praise me." I was uptight emotionally and spiritually. I wasn't free. As soon as I gave God a little bit of permission, the Holy Spirit did the rest Himself.

THE HOLY SPIRIT
HEALS US
HE WILL BRING TO LIGHT WHAT IS HIDDEN IN DARKNESS (1 CORINTHIANS 4:5)

Our experience in Toronto sparked a transformation in our lives back home. God had a lot more he wanted to do in our marriage. After several powerful encounters with the Holy Spirit, secrets that we had kept hidden for years finally came to light. We also learned from firsthand experience that there are unseen spiritual forces all around us. When we hold onto secrets, we stay oppressed spiritually. When we practice forgiveness and let God into every area of our lives, we can be set free.

MARIANNE: When we got back from Toronto, everything felt different for me spiritually. We prayed more together. We invited the Holy Spirit's presence to come, and we felt lighthearted, joyful, and had more desire than usual to read the Bible and pray for others. Before, my friends said that I had a 1,000-yard stare. If I wasn't engaged in the conversation, I would stare off into space, checked-out. After the trip to Toronto, my depression lifted. I smiled at people more – so much more that my friends started to notice. "What's going on with Marianne?" They asked Chuck. "Something's different about her."

I found I had a new enthusiasm for my work. It was the summertime, and I was just getting my class lists for the next year. In the past I had always told myself, "I should pray over my class list." But I never did anything about it. This time, I got really excited about praying for every kid on the list. Saying, "I should do something" and really doing it are two different things. After Toronto I actually wanted to start praying, and I was motivated to do it. So, I started praying through my class lists. I remember one really significant conversation with a kid in my class that resulted from prayer. His dad was sick. He came and talked to me about it. I told him about Jesus. It was really special, and it never would have happened without the filling of the Holy Spirit.

I didn't stop my prayers with the class lists. During my free time, on my breaks between classes, I would go through the halls and just ask the Holy Spirit to come fill up the place. It changed my whole experience of work, and it changed things for the people around me too. There was a coworker whom I had known for a while. She was a secular Muslim. One day after school she had a terrible headache. So, I asked her if I could pray for her. I hadn't done that sort of thing before, just asking if I could pray for someone right at that moment. There was a woman in our small group who used to pray for everybody at her work, and I really admired that about her. I'd thought, "That's so neat. I just don't know if I would ever do that." But after my experience in Toronto, I had more boldness. So, when this gal came into the staff room with a bad headache, I said, "Do you want me to pray for you?" It was only she and I in the room together. "Oh sure, you can pray for me," she said. So, I prayed that the headache would go away in Jesus' name. A few minutes later, she said, "It's gone. It's gone! My headache's gone! That never happens!" I thought, "Wow, that's pretty cool." It was only thanks to the Holy Spirit that I was able to do things like that. It was completely new for me.

After coming back from Toronto, Chuck and I started doing our mornings differently. We would put on worship music, and we either danced around or stood inviting the Holy Spirit to come. We were just reenacting what we had seen and experienced in Toronto. When we prayed with each other in our living room, the Holy Spirit would show up, and we would feel close to God. It was a big change in our marriage, because we were both feeling the same thing at the same time. But the biggest change was still yet to come.

Even though Jesus was renewing our love for each other, there was still something I had been hiding from Chuck. The secret kept me from being totally free. I had told Chuck about the kiss with my coworker at Christmastime some years back. What I hadn't told Chuck is that the relationship didn't end there. I knew that having an affair was wrong. But I had been hell-bent on doing the wrong thing anyway because I was just so angry at Chuck. My bitterness and longing drove me to do something I'd thought I would never do. There's a verse in the Bible that describes how bad feelings can turn into bad actions. "Watch out that no poisonous root of bitterness grows up to trouble you, corrupting many" (Hebrews 12:15). My root of bitterness had turned into a prolonged affair that spelled real trouble for my marriage.

By the time Chuck and I traveled to Toronto, I had ended the relationship with this man. But I'd never told Chuck how far it had gone. I had a girlfriend who was not a person of faith who said to me, "You can't ever tell Chuck. It'll ruin everything." So, I wasn't planning to tell him. Ever. At least, I hadn't been planning to tell him until God made it painfully clear that the truth had to come out. A year after our first trip to Toronto, we went back up there for a conference called "The Fire of God." I didn't know what the Fire of God meant at first. Thankfully, there was a speaker at the conference who explained it really well. "The fire of God is like the refiner's fire," he said. "This is how a metal refiner works. He takes the dirty mess of silver or gold ore and lights a flame under it. In the heat of the flame, the impurities in the ore float to the top, where the refiner can scrape them off. Then what's left is the pure gold or silver – so pure he can look into it and see his reflection. Through outpourings of the Holy Spirit," the speaker explained, "the Fire of God can purify us. Our impurities will rise to the top and be skimmed off. Then God can see His reflection in us." That made a lot of sense to me. Excited for more of God, I went to get prayer to receive the Fire of God.

A couple of people prayed for me, and I was feeling pretty good. Then a man on the prayer team came up to me and asked, "Can I pray for you?" "Okay," I said, "I already got prayer, but you can pray for me again." I was wearing heels, and when this man started praying for me, I started bobbing up and down really fast. Chuck saw me from a few feet away and thought, "This is looking wild! I'd better get over there!" As soon as Chuck got behind me, I shot backwards, like out of a cannon. Chuck caught me before I hit the ground. It was nuts. This Fire of God thing turned out to be really powerful. I didn't know what was happening at the time, but God was doing something to purify me on the inside.

I felt pretty good afterwards, until we were driving home from Toronto. Then, in the car, God spoke into my mind the exact words I never wanted to hear. "You've got to tell Chuck." "No," I said to the voice in my mind, "I'm not telling him." I would never tell Chuck about the affair. In his mind it had just been a kiss. Learning the truth would only hurt him. Not only that, it risked erasing all the good things that God was doing in our marriage. "This has to be from the enemy," I thought. "I'm not telling Chuck." We drove a little bit longer and I heard it again. "You have to tell Chuck." I thought, "Nope. No, no, no, no, no." A third time I heard it, and a third time I said, "No, I'm not doing it." Then Chuck suddenly felt something in his stomach. His whole body hunched over as if he were doing a stomach crunch. "I think God is trying to tell us something!" he said through clenched muscles. "Oh no," I thought. "I guess that *was* God prompting me." By this time, I was getting a splitting headache.

We had to drive onto a ferry to take the car across the lake. On the ferry, I sat down with Chuck and told him the truth. It had been a whole year of moving forward in our marriage. Chuck thought we were doing great. This new information devastated him. After we got off the ferry, my headache was worse. We started the drive home, and I asked Chuck to stop somewhere to get Advil. When we pulled up to a rest stop, I thought I was going to throw up. I got out of the car and started dry heaving. But nothing physical came out of me. Instead, I felt something else leave, something spiritual. I don't know what it was. A spirit of deception? A spirit of lust? All I know is that after finally revealing the truth to Chuck, something negative left my body in a physical way. Chuck came out of the store with a little bottle of Advil. He also had a rose which he'd bought inside the rest stop. "I forgive you, Marianne" he said. I didn't feel like I deserved to be forgiven, but I said, "Thank you." I took the rose from Chuck. At that moment I realized I didn't need the Advil. My headache was gone.

When people make fun of revivals or spectacular manifestations of the Holy Spirit, I say, "You just don't know." I didn't know how God would heal my marriage. I probably never would have said yes to Him if I did. It took several strange encounters with the Holy Spirit to make the truth come out and set everything right. You don't know what God's plan is for you. You don't know what the Holy Spirit will do when you let Him in. You just have to take the leap and say, "Yes. Okay, God." After I told Chuck the whole truth, and he forgave me, God paved the way for complete healing between us. It didn't happen overnight. We had a lot of talks after that day. We went to counseling and continued to work on our relationship. Exposing my secret allowed our intimate relationship to recover and improve. While we were being healed ourselves, God gave us opportunities to help other people heal, too. The next phase of our lives saw us engaged in full-time ministry. We prayed for many people and taught others how to open their hearts to pray for miraculous healings. It turns out that when you're hungry for more, God gives you more, even more than you could possibly ask for or imagine.

MOVING INTO FULL-TIME MINISTRY
THOSE AWESOME WONDERS YOU SAW WITH YOUR OWN EYES (DEUTERONOMY 10:21)

As we progressed in our ministry, we learned more about praying for healing. We began to teach others about the Holy Spirit. And then a new job opportunity supercharged our ministry to reach many more people.

CHUCK: After several trips to Toronto, I threw myself whole-heartedly into learning about the work of the Holy Spirit. I got a master's degree in ministry from The Peter Wagner Institute focused on the Holy Spirit. I went back and forth to Toronto for training, a total of eighteen times.

We transitioned from the Baptist church we had been attending to a Vineyard church where they were more open to signs and wonders. At our new church we received a lot of training on how to pray for the sick, how to hear from God, how to do deliverance, and how to help people experience the Holy Spirit. The most exciting learning opportunities came on the front lines, on mission trips to Brazil. There the experienced prayer team taught Marianne and me how to pray for miracles of healing.

In the Bible, Jesus prayed for the sick and they got healed. His disciples did, too, Peter and Paul, among others. But today most of us think, "I guess Jesus did that back then, but that was then, and this is now. Plus, I'm not Jesus." That sort of pessimism towards miracles goes against everything written about healing in the Bible. Here's what Jesus actually said: "I tell you the truth, anyone who believes in me will do the same works I have done, and even greater works, because I am going to be with the Father. You can ask for anything in my name, and I will do it, so that the Son can bring glory to the Father. Yes, ask me for anything in my name, and I will do it!" (John 14:12-14). Because we believe in Jesus, it is possible to see the same miracles today that Jesus performed in biblical times. We are to ask for them in Jesus' name. What's more, because Jesus went to the cross and conquered sin and death, restoring life to a dead creation, and then went to be with His Father and then sent the Holy Spirit into his disciples, He says that we can do even greater things than He did.

This takes some practice. It's hard to go from zero to miracles of healing if you've never seen one before. The prayer team in Brazil helped us by modeling their faith and by giving us a method for praying for the sick. First, interview the person about what's going on. "How can I pray for you?" You can also ask, "How much is the pain on a scale of one to ten?" This gives you a benchmark. After you've prayed for them, you can ask again how high the pain number is. If the number has gone down, it encourages you both. Then you just pray in Jesus' name. You speak to the condition and say, "Be healed in Jesus' name." You can pray specific things like, "Knee cartilage, be healed in Jesus' name." "All scar tissue go, in Jesus' name." "Pain leave, in Jesus' name." After you pray short direct prayers, ask again how the person is feeling. If there was no change, check in and ask a question, such as, "Is there anyone you need to forgive related to your condition?" If there was improvement, thank God and point out where the healing is coming from. "Hey, Jesus is doing this! Thank you, God!"

One of the main reasons Jesus commanded his disciples to heal the sick was to show people what God's kingdom is ultimately like. "Go and announce to them that the Kingdom of Heaven is near," Jesus said as he sent out his followers. "Heal the sick, raise the dead, cure those with leprosy, and cast out demons" (Matthew 10:7-8). There is no sickness in God's Heaven. There we will be well. We believe this with all our hearts. And still, every time we see a miracle it's surprising and exciting.

On Marianne's first trip to Brazil, she prayed for a woman's knee. Not two seconds after Marianne started praying, the woman exclaimed, "Oh!" and started walking around like her knee was fine. Marianne thought, "Are you sure you're okay?" She was just so surprised that the prayer worked. One young Brazilian girl Marianne prayed for had lumps all over her chest. Marianne prayed for her, commanding the lumps to go away in Jesus' name. Later Marianne saw the girl again in the bathroom. The girl said, "It's all better, I can't feel any of the lumps!" She lifted up her shirt to show Marianne. "Are you sure?" Marianne asked. Marianne hadn't really expected anything to happen. Thank God it didn't matter whether Marianne expected it to work or not! She just prayed in the name of Jesus, and the girl was healed.

The more healings we witnessed, the more we came to expect them. One of the first times I prayed for someone in Brazil, the guy started acting really strangely. He was shaking and looking very uncomfortable. I didn't know what to do. Someone on the prayer team came by and said, "Just tell it to go in Jesus' name." Obediently I said, "In the name of Jesus, get out of him now, afflicting spirit!" At that moment I literally saw something ripple through that man. Like a shudder, it went down his arm, and then out of him completely. As it left, the guy got thrown back onto the floor. When he got up, he had total peace. Everything was fine.

Because of this experience, we began to deal with afflicting spirits back home. If you're praying for someone and their pain gets stronger, or if the pain starts moving, it could be an afflicting spirit. In Jesus' name you can take authority over spirits and tell them to go. This is often necessary in emotional healing, too. When a person has been hurt in the past, or sinned deliberately, a spirit can stick to them and continue to cause trouble. When I was working through my own personal healing, I talked a lot about my relationship with my father and the pain and anger I still felt towards him. One day, with the help of a counselor, I was praying a prayer of forgiveness for my father, releasing him from my judgement to receive God's blessing. Suddenly I felt something leave me. I opened my mouth like I needed to yawn, but it was something else. Something left right after I forgave my father. Then I felt peaceful. All that is to say there's a lot more going on in the spiritual world than we can possibly understand. This is what the Bible reminds us of. "We are not fighting against flesh-and-blood enemies, but against evil rulers and authorities of the unseen world, against mighty powers in this dark world, and against evil spirits in the heavenly places" (Ephesians 6:12).

Through the extended prayer process, God showed me that when I was around four or five, and my dad had come back home from the war, I didn't run to him and hug him. I didn't know him at all. To me he was only a photo on the dresser. I realized then through prayer, that that little boy hadn't bonded with his dad because his dad was away for most of his young life. When my dad returned, it felt as though he took my mom away from me. I had to forgive him for that. I also had to ask God to forgive me for my disrespect, and for pushing him away. It took me a long time to recognize that I needed to forgive my dad for all that I had held in my heart against him. Then I could truly appreciate all that he had done for me and for our family.

We had lots of fun times together; hiking, camping, playing football. My dad was supportive and came to my sporting events and other school activities. He and my mom even sold their home in Walnut Creek to move with us to Isla Vista to be part of our home church movement. When my dad died at the age of eighty-nine, I was honored to speak at his funeral service and I was able to bless him.

Praying for healing – both physical and emotional – became a big part of my ministry after I retired from teaching. Marianne and I traveled around the country teaching classes on how to pray for healing. Our friends Steve and Starla whom we hadn't seen in thirty years asked us to speak at their church Marysville, Washington. We went out and shared our story about healing in our marriage and about hearing from God. While we were visiting Marysville, we ran into a woman from our old church group who had herself experienced a life change as a result of an encounter with the Holy Spirit. Now she had a prophetic ministry, where she told people encouraging things that she heard God saying. She offered to speak into a cassette tape for Marianne and me. We were all sitting in the car together in front of a park, and she just started talking into this recorder. She talked and talked for over twenty minutes. Some of the things she said were personal, things we couldn't believe she knew. One of the things she said was particularly encouraging for our work. "I see you guys behind a horse and plow," she said. "You've been plowing along, working hard for God. So far, you've just been plowing little fields, because you just had one little plow. But I see that changing. I see you in a John Deere tractor, with air conditioning and big, huge plows behind it. From now on you're going to be plowing big fields, and it's going to be much more relaxing."

Not long after that I got a phone call that would lead to an opportunity to dramatically expand our ministry. Dave Schmelzer and his wife Grace had started a Vineyard church in Boston. Our son Andrew had joined the pastoral staff team, and by now the church had rapidly grown from thirty people meeting in a living room to around one thousand people on any given Sunday. The church was looking for more pastors to work full time on inner healing and prayer ministry. Andrew recommended Marianne and me. "How would you like to come to Boston?" Dave asked. It was a great opportunity for us. For one thing, it meant that I could finally get paid for the work I felt God was calling me to do. For another thing, it meant we could live and work close to our son Andrew, his wife Val, and their family. We moved down to Boston, and before we knew it the prophesy from our friend in Washington was coming true. The church started to grow into one of the few mega churches in the Boston area. Over the next many years, we saw hundreds of lives transformed through the power of the Holy Spirit. We ran weekly healing rooms where anybody could stop in to get prayer for physical ailments. We ran weekend-long workshops where participants dove into inner healing. It really was as if we were coasting through our work riding in the air-conditioned cab of a big John Deere tractor.

TRAGEDY STRIKES AGAIN

YOU WILL HAVE MANY TRIALS AND SORROWS (JOHN 16:33)

After losing our daughter Amy so many years before, we had thought we'd learned all there was to know about suffering and loss. We were wrong. Seven years into our work in Boston, our son Andrew was diagnosed with stage four colon cancer. We believed in miraculous healing, and we did everything we could think of to try to get Andrew well. In this trying time, we learned anew that God is always with us. God is always for us. And we need Him more than ever.

CHUCK: Working in the ministry with our son Andrew was amazing. I got to see him nearly every day. One of our favorite things to do was to sit in a coffee shop and talk about small groups. We'd strategize about how to meet new people and how to help them.

Andrew had always been a great kid. One reason that we

clicked was that he was a people person, just like me. He loved building relationships – especially relationships where everyone could be honest and open with each other. Even as a high schooler, Andrew read books about counseling and inner healing. Andrew always wanted to talk about the tough stuff. He would push us into deep conversations, but he brought it up in a nice way, so we didn't feel offended. At Stanford, Andrew got involved with the Intervarsity Christian Fellowship. There he met his wife, Val and both of them moved to Boston to be part of this new growing church.

Technically, Andrew was my boss, but it didn't feel that way. It just felt great to be with him and to bond over the work we both loved. We did that for nearly seven years. Because Andrew and I were working together every day, I sometimes heard him complaining about his stomach. His stomach would often bother him, and he said, "I'm probably getting an ulcer or something." I don't know if he ever mentioned to me that he'd found blood in his stools, but I do remember that one day he said, "I'm going to go get a checkup." He called me on the phone the day after Saint Patrick's Day 2008. "Dad," Andrew said, "I have stage four colon cancer." Then he started crying.

I just couldn't believe what I was hearing. Stage four colon cancer is like a death sentence. Nobody survives it beyond five years. Hearing someone say they have stage four colon cancer is like hearing somebody died, but they're still alive and talking to you. Marianne and I didn't know how to process the news. We were both stunned. But we didn't have much time to process. The doctors were all over Andrew immediately. In the first operation they cut out a foot of his colon. They also removed his omentum, because the cancer had spread to there too. Andrew said jokingly, "They took out my omentum. I guess I didn't need it that much." He made light of the situation as much as he could. He even gave a sermon about it after he got diagnosed. But in reality, he was fighting for his life. He lost forty pounds in the two months following the operation. Then he needed a second operation. In a short time, Andrew went from a 36-year-old who could run fast to a hunched-over sick man who could barely walk.

While Marianne helped out with the kids and Val took Andrew to appointments, I had my own job: figuring out how to get Andrew prayer for miraculous healing. Remember, Marianne and I were the prayer ministry pastors at our church. So, we obviously were champions of praying for healing. The whole church came together in multiple ways to pray for Andrew. They held big meetings in the church building where everybody prayed together. Small groups prayed every week in different areas of the city. Individuals fasted as a way of asking God for a miracle. We also got giants of the faith to come pray for him. Heidi Baker, a well-known missionary from Mozambique, came to our church several times. On one visit she prayed with us in our living room. On another visit Heidi went to Andrew's hospital room to pray for him. There was a man I met at a conference who had seen miraculous physical healings in Uganda. Somebody at the church donated $2000 to pay for his flight from Africa to come to America. He came to our church and taught a workshop, and he stayed in our house and prayed for Andrew three nights in a row.

We also sent Andrew off to places where people were reporting miraculous healing. One of these places was in Northern California. The story of Andrew getting there was simply paved with miraculous coincidences. First Andrew called the church to ask where he could stay in the area. The person who picked up the phone happened to be an old friend of mine to whom I had talked about Jesus way back when we were in college together. In those days he hadn't been interested in Jesus at all. But many years later, his wife had gotten miraculously healed, and he had found Jesus. Now my old college buddy was there answering the phones. When Andrew explained about his cancer, my old friend said, "Why don't you come and stay with us?" Andrew traveled to Northern California and stayed at my friend's home. After a powerful experience in a prayer service there,

Andrew thought he might be healed from his cancer. He went back to the house and wrote all about it in my friend's guest book. But despite the encouraging signs, Andrew wasn't healed of his cancer that night.

I took Andrew to Kansas City, to the International House of Prayer where people had reported some amazing healings taking place. The coincidence stories piled up on this trip too. The plane we were on stopped in Milwaukee before the final leg of the trip. Suddenly the captain came over the loudspeaker and said, "Sorry, we've got a problem. Everybody needs to get off the plane." This hardly ever happens, but we all got off the plane and shuttled back into the airport. Just as I stepped into the terminal, I saw someone walking down the hallway towards us. It was the man from Uganda who had come to pray for Andrew just a month before. What were the chances? I ran up to him and said, "I think it's a sign. Will you pray for Andrew again?" He said, "I don't have much time, but I'll pray for Andrew right now." So right there in the airport, he stopped and prayed for Andrew. We both felt like: "This is it. This is when the miracle is going to happen." But Andrew wasn't healed of his cancer that day.

We finally flew to Kansas City where there was a church in the midst of revival. It was one huge meeting after another, but Andrew was so weak he couldn't walk to the front of the church. Thankfully, we knew someone on staff at the church, and we had all these connections in the world of prayer healing. Every famous prayer minister there came to Andrew one by one to pray for him. Meanwhile, at the front of the church, someone got up on stage and said, "Last night I got healed from stage four colon cancer. In this room." We all thought: "This is confirmation. Andrew's getting healed now." But Andrew wasn't healed of his cancer in Kansas City.

We went to Florida, and to Georgia. Other well-known prayer ministers visited our church and stayed in our house. Hundreds of people from all around the world prayed and fasted for Andrew's cancer to be cured. We kept cheering, "Miracle! Miracle! Miracle!" But despite all the signs of God's love, Andrew wasn't healed. Instead, he got sicker and sicker. He soberly prepared the people around him. He wrote letters for his three boys to open on their birthdays. And he continued to think of the people around him, including me. "Does Dad really understand that I'm probably going to die?" Andrew asked Val the last time he was in the hospital. He was worried about me spiritually. I did know he would probably die. But I kept thinking, "Maybe he can get a miracle." Even on my last night with him, I was still praying. But it didn't happen. Andrew died at home in the morning.

Val called me and asked if I could pick up the older two boys at school. She told me not to tell them anything specific. Not that I could have said anything anyway. She said to just pick them up and bring them home. I drove to the elementary school and walked into the school office. It got very quiet in there. The staff of the school all knew what was happening, and they ran and got the boys right away. The kids didn't ask me any questions. But as they sat in the car, the five-year-old turned to the eight-year-old and started talking. "I wonder why Papa's here?" he said, using the name they called me. "I don't think we have a dentist's appointment." "I don't remember Mom saying anything about a doctor's appointment." They kept going back and forth, wondering aloud what was going on. But they didn't ask me one question. I just thought, "These poor boys. Their dad just died." It was so unfair.

Processing Andrew's death felt more complicated than dealing with Amy's. With Amy, we mourned that she didn't get a chance to live. She was so vivacious and eager, and her life got cut short so early. But Andrew's death was a tragedy that rippled across so many lives. He had a wife and three young boys. We grieved for Andrew because he wasn't here anymore. But we also had to grieve for his young family and for the effect that his death would have on their whole lives. Andrew's death also had a huge effect on the church in

Boston.

And we grieved for ourselves as well. Marianne and I had lost two children. How much could life possibly throw at us? How could we ever feel normal again? We got involved with a support group of other parents who had also lost children. That helped us a lot. We were also supported by friends who would always take our calls, no matter what time of the day or night. And our church community was a huge comfort. Andrew's funeral was unbelievable. The place was packed out. Walking down the aisle behind the casket, I saw people who had flown in from all over the country. Church members cut short international vacations to be at Andrew's funeral. The line of cars going across town to the cemetery was so long that the police couldn't keep up with it.

On the Sunday following Andrew's death, our friend Grace faced the difficult task of saying something to our devastated church congregation. She preached from 2 Corinthians; a letter written to a church in suffering. In 2 Corinthians, the author of the letter was writing to people he had loved, taught, shared life with, and brought into relationship with Christ. He says, "The only letter of recommendation we need is you yourselves. Your lives are a letter written in our hearts; everyone can read it and recognize our good work among you" (2 Corinthians 3:2). In her sermon, Grace talked about the good work Andrew had done during his lifetime – what he might put into a letter of recommendation. He had worked tirelessly loving people, teaching in the church, sharing in weddings and small groups, and helping people grow closer to God. At the end of her talk, Grace asked the people gathered in church that Sunday, "If you were personally touched by Andrew in some way, please stand up now." Nearly everyone stood up. "Your lives," Grace said, "are Andrew's letters of recommendation." Standing at the back of the church, I watched all those people stand up. I was overcome by feelings of pride, awe and gratitude of a life well lived.

When Marianne and I struggled with questions of

"Why?" there were some books that helped us understand. Our favorite titles are included in an appendix at the end of this book. One theologian in particular helped us put Andrew's death in perspective. In his books Greg Boyd takes apart the notion that everything that happens to us is part of God's plan. If you look at the Bible closely, not everything that happens is God's will. There's a lot of heinous stuff that goes on. Jesus even warned his disciples about it. "Here on earth you will have many trials and sorrows. But take heart, because I have overcome the world" (John 16:33). Most of Jesus' disciples died young. They suffered terrible deaths. Jesus didn't want it that way. He loved them. But there are forces in the world that defy God's will. The Bible says so. "We are not fighting against flesh-and-blood enemies, but against evil rulers and authorities of the unseen world, against mighty powers in this dark world, and against evil spirits in the heavenly places" (Ephesians 6:12).

When Marianne read Boyd's book, her experiences finally made sense to her. God didn't cause tragedy to happen. He never wanted any of it. After Amy's death, people often said to Marianne, "Maybe it was God's will. Maybe if Amy had lived in the States and hadn't moved to Europe, she would have fallen out of a tree or something." Marianne always thought, "What a horrible thing to say!" After reading Boyd's book, Marianne felt assured that the deaths of our children were never God's will. God is always good. As Boyd explains, the world is complex. There are powers at play that we can't understand. And there are people with free will, evading the will of God. Sometimes we see miracles, and sometimes we don't. Why? It's a mystery. But the mystery is not about God. The mystery is about us, about the forces that surround us, and about God's timeline for defeating those forces.

Boyd closes his book with an incredibly hopeful thought. The Bible has the audacity to say that everything we're going through now, all our grief and pain, will pale in comparison to the glory we'll experience when we see God again. "Our present troubles are small and won't last very long. Yet they produce for us a glory that vastly outweighs them and will last forever!" (2 Corinthians 4:17) Cancer and death. Loss of children. The Bible claims that one day, when we finally see all the good that God has in store for us, these will seem to us like momentary speed bumps on God's highway of glory. That's a crazy thought. But that's what the Bible says. It's a hope that's kept us from going crazy.

In addition to good friends and good books, our main and most important source of comfort since Andrew's death has been the presence of the Holy Spirit who is the very presence of Jesus. After Amy died, the Holy Spirit gave Marianne's mother a dream about Amy in heaven. After Andrew died, both Marianne and I had prophetic dreams that reassured us Andrew was okay. Marianne's dream happened just a few months after Andrew's death. She was grieving powerfully in those days, and when she was alone in the house she would really let loose with sobbing and wailing. In her dream, Marianne saw Andrew sitting at a big oak table in our neighborhood library. He looked healthy in a blue and white striped shirt. Andrew turned to Marianne and said, "Mom!" It was as if he'd said, "Mom! Come on! Get a hold of yourself! Look, I'm fine." The message Marianne took from that dream was that Andrew was okay. Although he was dead, he was alive somewhere. And she didn't need to go crazy in her grief. I had a similar dream. I saw Andrew in the same public library. The same brown oak table. The same blue and white shirt. And he looked great. These experiences, beyond anything our friends could say or anything we could read in a book, told us on a gut level that God had everything in His hands. He had more for us than we could understand or imagine, and we were going to be okay.

There's a reason that the Bible calls the Holy Spirit "The Comforter." Even in the wake of the double tragedy of losing two children, we have never wanted to give up our trust in God. Every time we call on the Holy Spirit, He comes. We feel God's presence, and we feel again that God is good. God is good to us. He stands with us as we experience both pain and joy. He encourages us that whatever our troubles, He has overcome them. And He always has more love to give.

OUR LIFE WITH GOD TODAY

TODAY WHEN YOU HEAR HIS VOICE,
DON'T HARDEN YOUR HEARTS
(HEBREWS 3:15)

Today life is good. We lean on the Holy Spirit as much as we ever did. We are still desperate for God. We need God every day. The Holy Spirit still has things to teach us. And we continue to reach for more.

CHUCK: Today we're just as desperate for God as we've been at any other time in our lives. For me, it starts first thing in the morning. I wake up in a fog, and I have no idea where I am. My first thought is, "Just get me to the bathroom!" And I have to climb down a staircase that's a little dangerous at my age. So, by necessity, I start off each day praying, "Jesus, I need you today." I say this prayer as I'm holding on to the railing, taking the steps one at a time. "Jesus, I need you today." That's my first connection with God each day.

My desperate need for God keeps me connected with Him on a daily basis. And I love it. During the course of my day, whenever I stop and say, "Holy Spirit come," He comes. Pretty soon I'm sensing Him. He's there. Jesus is really with us now, and we can feel Him. We can experience Him. He's right here, right now. And the Holy Spirit still surprises me. Here's a recent story.

A couple of years ago, Marianne and I were driving from our home in Boston to see our grandkids in Portland, Maine, when our Toyota Camry began making the kind of engine noises that you hope never to hear. We were about twenty minutes from our daughter's house, but we were too scared to finish the trip with the screaming engine. After some frantic phone calls, we reached a friend in Maine who recommended a good local mechanic. We had the car towed to his shop, which was closed at the time, and we got a lift to our daughter's house. When I talked to the mechanic over the phone, I learned that the car engine was ruined and would need to be replaced. It would cost $4,000 and take about a week to complete. All that money and a week without a car? What a blow! "Oh well," I thought. "What else can I do?" I said yes to the mechanic, and a week later we were driving home in a Toyota Camry that felt 65,000 miles newer.

Three months later I took the car to my mechanic in Boston for an oil change. It was then that I got a terrible shock. The newly replaced engine was cracked and needed replacing again! Furious, I called the guy in Maine right away. He apologized and told me he would take full responsibility for redoing the repair. All I had to do was drive two hours up to Buxton, Maine, leave the car with him, take the bus home, and reverse the trip in another few days. This was not the way I wanted to spend my week, but I sighed and made the appointment anyway. At least the mechanic told me that the insurance would cover the cost of the repair.

When the car was ready to pick up again, I got a call on

my voicemail. The car was all set, he told me. He just needed $150 for the repair. "A hundred and fifty dollars??! Are you kidding me?" I yelled as I listened to the phone message. "I already gave you $4,000, spent two weeks without a car, and drove four hours back and forth to Maine!" There was no way I was going to pay another $150. This guy was taking advantage of me. I called him back, determined to stand my ground. When I got him on the phone, I told him I didn't want to pay any additional money for the botched engine repair. He was hesitant as he explained to me the costs he faced. There had been a few additional parts he had to cover, plus the price of oil. I could tell that it was difficult for him to ask for the $150. I responded in a calm tone (the first time) that I had already paid him $4,000. I'd gone two weeks without a car and traveled back and forth to Maine to work with him. He should have told me earlier about the added cost. Again, he enumerated his costs adding up to $150. Again, I listed my rights and complaints. This went back and forth at least five times. Each time my voice got more heated with emotion. Finally, I said, "Okay, I'll split the difference with you. We'll each pay $75. I'm not happy with this, but I need my car back and you've got me over a barrel." He still didn't budge. So I reluctantly went ahead and paid the whole thing with my credit card.

I hung up the phone feeling furious. If there's one thing I hate, it's the feeling that someone is taking advantage of me. Marianne was next to me when I'd made the call, and she'd heard my end of the conversation. "You know," Marianne said, "You were calm and firm the first time you explained yourself, but by the fourth and fifth time, you sounded pretty intense." That's when I knew this wasn't just about the car. This was an old spiritual issue coming back to haunt me. Being taken advantage of is a big fear for me, especially when it comes to money. I had felt pushed regarding finances by the leader of our former church in Maine. An investment scheme had bilked me out of my retirement savings. I wasn't just reacting to this mechanic over the phone. I was reacting to hurts I'd experienced decades before.

That night in my sleep God nudged me. "Let it go, Chuck. Forgive the mechanic." "Jesus," I prayed in my dream, "thank you for dying in my place that I might be forgiven. I choose to forgive those who have hurt me or sinned against me. I forgive the mechanic for asking for $150. I give him unconditional forgiveness. He owes me nothing. I entrust him to you, God, and I bless him in your name." Next, God prompted me that I needed to ask for forgiveness, too. I had been angry and judgmental. So, I prayed, "God, I ask you to forgive me for my ungodly response of anger and judgment. Thank you, Jesus, that I am forgiven and that you are setting me free." But God still wasn't done with me! "Chuck," God added, "To show you've really forgiven, I want you to write the mechanic a nice note blessing him. And give him $50 cash, in addition to the $150 you already paid." "What?!" I responded. "God, this is so unfair!" But when I woke up, I knew it was God. And God is always right.

I had a $50 bill stowed away in a special place in a drawer. I took out the bill, and I got a card. I wrote a nice note apologizing to the mechanic for my part in the argument. In the note, I blessed the mechanic and his family. Then I put the $50 in the envelope and sealed it up.

The following Monday my daughter Ingrid, who had been visiting us in Boston, drove me to Portland, Maine. My sister took me the rest of the way to the repair shop in Buxton. The shop was closed on Mondays, but the mechanic had left the keys for me inside the car. With my card for him in my hand, I looked through the window of the car. I saw something lying on the front seat. It was a white envelope with my name on it. I opened the envelope from him. It contained $75 and a note from the mechanic apologizing for the way he had acted over the phone. I couldn't believe it. For a moment I sat alone in my car holding both notes of apology. I cried. God had spoken to both of us. I took my sealed envelope with the $50 bill inside and wrote on the outside, "This is hilarious!" Then I dropped it into the mailbox outside his shop.

The next day I received a text from the mechanic. "Hi Chuck. Thank you for the card. You are too generous, and you did not need to give us the money. I am sorry for how I treated you, and I realized I was wrong after we spoke on the phone. Thank you so much, and let us know if you need anything. Take care, and yes, God Bless you and your family as well." God continues to humble me. And as I listen to Him, God shows me that miracles are possible, in my heart and in other people's hearts, too. I am grateful that my car works beautifully now. But I am even more grateful at how beautifully my life works out when I listen to God, especially when I fail again, and He gently calls me to own it long enough to be forgiven and freed from it, as in Romans 2:4.

Like the quick note I wrote on the outside of that envelope, it's hilarious. Of all the things I've learned in my years following God, perhaps the biggest lesson is to not take myself too seriously. When Marianne and I met, God had me humorously dropping peanuts into a soda. And when God gave Marianne and me renewal in our marriage, it started with laughter. Up in Toronto, the spirit of laughter was on everybody. I remember walking outside of the church one afternoon to get a hot dog for lunch. There were these two guys who had each bought a hot dog, and they were trying to eat, but they couldn't stop laughing. There they were, sitting with these hot dogs piled with onions and pickles and mustard, and they couldn't get the things into their mouths. They were just laughing too hard.

Today, Marianne and I make it a practice to not take ourselves too seriously. There's a TV show about lawyers, and there's one tough judge in that show. This judge makes the lawyers come up to the bench and give their arguments. After they go on and on with their "blah blah blah," the judge corrects them by saying, "In your opinion." Then the lawyer has to say: "In my opinion, blah blah blah." This has become a joke between Marianne and me. Whenever one of us makes a bold declaration, "This is the way things have to be!" The other one of us says, "In your opinion." Then we both just break out laughing.

There are other things we say to keep life light-hearted. When we have a family event and it's about time for everybody to go home, I'll start to sing "The Party's Over" by Willie Nelson. My daughter-in-law Val even looked up all the words to the song so I could sing the whole thing. Or I'll quote the character from the movie "Never Cry Wolf," who doesn't have any teeth. He smiles his big toothless grin and says, "Good idea!" So, if I'm in the middle of an argument with Marianne, I'll cover up my teeth with my lips and say, "Good idea!" That cuts the tension pretty quickly. God doesn't want us to take ourselves too seriously. He's clearly got a sense of humor.

MARIANNE: My relationship with Chuck is really good today. So is my relationship with God. When I went through hard times in my life, I never stopped believing in Jesus, but I wasn't having any kind of an active relationship with him, either. Now that's changed. I find myself talking to God a lot more often than I ever used to. Of course, I can always choose to be in a funk if I want to. I have free will. God never overrides anyone's free will. I think the Holy Spirit is always working with everybody, but each person has the choice to listen or not to listen. Some people say, "I don't care, I'm going to do the wrong thing anyway." Or they might not be thinking at all – they're so far down that track. For me, that explains how bad things can happen in a world where God is supposed to be good. He's good, but people have to choose His goodness.

I still have to choose to listen to God to hear his voice. It's not so different from choosing to listen in my marriage with Chuck. I have to sit down and make time for it. Sometimes Chuck will come home from his day's activities and I'll start shouting questions at him from up the stairs. He's one floor below me and I'm one floor above him, and

I'm trying to yell a conversation. Chuck will say to me, "Love, let's get together. Let's have a cup of tea and talk." So, we'll sit down at the same table and talk about our day. Then we can really listen to each other. It's much better that way.

Today I take a lot of joy in my family. My daughter Ingrid and I are like two peas in a pod. We both love thrift shopping and gardening. We talk often on the phone since she lives two hours away. Ingrid majored in Math in college, and then started her career working with Retirement plans. She started as an analyst and is now a consultant. She works hard at her job and loves being a wife and a mother to three children. Most of all I'm happy she has a relationship with Jesus. She and her husband, Chris, are leaders in their church community and enjoy hosting small groups in their home. Occasionally she volunteers for mission trips. She's traveled to Ecuador and Haiti.

I love being with Ingrid's and with Val's families. We have a lot of fun together. There's one picture of all of us sitting in our living room wearing matching Norwegian sweaters. It was Ingrid's idea to put everyone in Norwegian sweaters, since our heritage is from Norway. We got the kids each a sweater and took the photo. My grandkids said they would die if we ever shared the photo with anyone, so I'm not allowed to make it public on social media. But I have the photograph framed in my living room. Every time I see that picture, I smile. And I pray for those kids.

I pray that they'll have their own encounter with God, where they meet Jesus personally.

I pray that they don't give up on God.

I pray that they'll know God is real.

I pray that they'll decide God is worth it.

From the hardships and mistakes in my own life, I

believe that God can turn anything around, no matter how broken your life is. No matter how much you've messed up, God loves you. You can turn to God and change. This was true for my dad, whom I used to wait up for when I was a kid, wondering if he would make it home from drinking. He stopped drinking at some point, and I had a talk with him about Jesus. Not long after Amy died, my dad came to see us in Belgium. This is what he said to me. "Mary, I haven't lived much of a Christian life. But I want to live the rest of my life so I can be able to go to heaven and see Amy when I die." One night after that my mom came into the TV room to see my dad watching Billy Graham on the television. Dad sat in his chair in front of the TV, and he prayed. He asked God to help him to receive Jesus. Because of my brother's death in WWII so many years before, my Dad had been hardened to God. But when Amy died something changed. He decided to try Jesus. He started reading his Bible. At the end of his life, my dad was a totally different person from the man I remembered growing up. It was really wonderful. What I've learned in my life is there's always more God can do. There's always more from the Holy Spirit.

1 John 5:6 says that the Spirit of God "is truth." For this reason, I don't recommend keeping secrets. Secrets separate you from the people you love most, and they separate you from God. Don't keep any secrets, whether it's an affair or money, or anything else. We're all a mess, and God isn't surprised by any of it. By seeking forgiveness, offering forgiveness, and asking God to transform us, we can be set free. It's not about going to Toronto or somewhere else, or not. It's not about living in close Christian community, or not. Who knows what opportunity the Holy Spirit will make available to you. The point is, if you feel a hunger for more of God, He wants to give His peace and His presence to you! We can constantly be made new because Jesus already did all the hard work. He did it all on the cross so that we can experience God's love. That's what the Holy Spirit told me when I fell on the ground in Toronto. "All I want to do is love you," I heard God say. I believe God just wants to love you, too.

APPENDIX: BOOKS WE LOVE
FURTHER READING ON THE HOLY SPIRIT

Here are some books we love with a description of how each one affected us and what we hope you'll learn from reading them.

On Suffering

Is God to Blame? Beyond Pat Answers to the Problem of Suffering by Gregory A. Boyd

Greg Boyd's book gave us a theological framework to understand our own suffering in the context of God's goodness. God is always good and is always against evil. God isn't to blame for our suffering. God is the one who walks us through suffering to new life.

On the Holy Spirit

The Presence & The Power: The significance of the Holy Spirit in the life and ministry of Jesus by Gerald F. Hawthorne

Working with Andrew for those eight and a half to nine years was one of the greatest highlights of my life. Even though Andrew was our son, he helped us spiritually. He encouraged us with words of affirmation. He often suggested different spiritual books for us to read. One book he liked was by Gordon Fee and was about the Apostle Paul and his dependence on the Holy Spirit.

As I was reading through Fee's book, I noticed a footnote referencing a Wheaton College professor, Gerald Hawthorne, and his book *The Presence and the Power*. It was out of print, but I found a used copy on the internet. I found this book to be encouraging because it helped me make sense out of some of my own experiences. It was all about how Jesus was fully human. (He was and is fully God, as well, but that is a different part of the story.) As a man, he was obedient and faithful to his father by the power of the Holy Spirit.

Here's a powerful quote from Hawthorne's book: "If indeed Jesus was God having become truly human, if indeed Jesus really experienced the same kinds of things that all other human beings experience, suffered the same kinds of pains they suffer, felt the same emotions they feel, knew the same lure of temptation they know, and so on, and if indeed Jesus stood strong against all the kaleidoscope adversities of human existence and resisted all the many pressures to cave in, quit, give up the cause, and go on his own way, and if indeed Jesus finally brought his God-given mission in life to a triumphant completion— and all of this because he was a person filled with the Spirit – then the followers of Jesus are faced with a stupendous fact: Not only is Jesus our Savior because of who he was and because of his own complete obedience to the father's will (Hebrews 10:5-7), but he is the supreme example for them of what is possible in human life because of his own total dependence upon the Spirit of God."

Reading this, it hit me again: Life, my life, is intended to be all about Jesus. He came to model a human life led and empowered by the Holy Spirit. And then He died, conquered death, rose again, and ascended to the Father in heaven so that the Father and He could send the Holy Spirit to be on us and in us so that we could live like He did as a man.

Paul, the Spirit, and the People of God by Gordon D. Fee

When he was only in High School, Andrew started reading Gordon Fee's work. Later, Andrew passed along some tapes by Gordon that made a big impression on our growing understanding of the Holy Spirit. According to this book, Paul is a model for what ministry can look like after Jesus released the Holy Spirit onto his disciples. Paul demonstrated that everyone who follows Jesus has access to the Holy Spirit.

There is More! The Secret to Experience God's Power to Change Your Life by Randy Clark

We traveled with Randy Clark on numerous mission trips to Brazil where he taught us firsthand how to pray for healing and deliverance. We love Randy's message that there's always more you can get from God: more joy, more power, and more experience of Him.

Birthing the Miraculous: The Power of Personal Encounters with God to Change Your Life and The World by Heidi Baker

Along with her husband Roland, Heidi Baker was a burned-out missionary who came to the renewal in Toronto, Canada around the same time we did. Heidi was touched by the Holy Spirit so powerfully that it completely changed her ministry. Now she has seen thousands of miracles of healing and planted many churches in Mozambique, Africa. Heidi Baker visited our church in Boston and prayed for Andrew twice. Any one of her books is a window onto a powerful relationship with the Holy Spirit.

When Heaven Invades Earth by Bill Johnson

Bill Johnson was a big influence on us when we were first trying to understand how to bring the Holy Spirit into our everyday lives. This book was inspiring and encouraging.

Holy Fire by R.T. Kendall

A balanced, biblical look at the Holy Spirit's work in our lives.

The Presence of God: Discovering God's Ways Through Intimacy with Him by R.T. Kendall

As we've gone through difficult periods in our lives, it's been harder than at other times to be intimate with God. R.T. Kendall explains that it's normal to sometimes feel God's presence powerfully, and to have difficulty sensing Him at other times. This book talks about ways to be more sensitive to God's presence and to deepen in relationship with Him.

Present Perfect: Finding God in the Now by Gregory A. Boyd

We're always moved by the way Greg Boyd puts complex theology into practical terms. This book gives tips on how to listen to the Holy Spirit in your day to day life.

Surprised by the Power of the Spirit: Discovering How God Speaks and Heals Today by Jack Deere
Surprised by the Voice of God: How God Speaks Today Through Prophecies, Dreams, and Visions by Jack Deere

Before we experienced the Holy Spirit, we were prejudiced against anybody who spoke in tongues or talked too much about the gifts of the Spirit. Jack Deere's books helped change our thinking. According to Jack Deere, visions and miracles aren't only for biblical times – the Bible makes a clear argument that we should be able to hear from God and see miracles today.

When the Spirit Comes with Power: Signs & Wonders among God's People by John White

Our experience in Toronto, Canada may have seemed crazy to other people at the time, but it shouldn't have been all that surprising. According to John White, revivals have been a normal part of the Christian experience throughout history. Our takeaway is that when we see people experiencing God in powerful ways, we should go after it!

The River Is Here: Receiving and Sustaining the Blessing of Revival by Melinda Fish

This little book by Melina Fish explains more about the revival in Toronto, Canada that had such a big effect on our lives. Melinda argues that what happened in Toronto has its basis in the Bible.

Open My Eyes, Lord by Gary Oates

In Toronto, Canada, our friend Gary got an amazing vision from the Holy Spirit. He describes his experience in this book. We even make an appearance in one chapter!

On Inner Healing

A Guide for Listening and Inner-Healing Prayer: Meeting God in the Broken Places by Rusty Rustenbach

In our lives we've found that inner healing needs to be an ongoing practice. This workbook gives you a framework that you can use to get free. We've used similar step-by-step instructions in the classes we teach on inner healing.

Deliverance from Evil Spirits by Francis MacNutt

When we started praying for other people and for our own inner healing, we found out that there is a vast spiritual realm we didn't see or understand. This book explains the spiritual side of deliverance and gives practical advice on how to pray for yourself and for others.

ABOUT THE AUTHORS

Chuck and Marianne love to share their story, present workshops on how to hear from God, how to pray for the sick, how to lead small groups, and how to get set free from past hurts.

Through their pastoring, and extended prayer ministry, Chuck and Marianne have helped hundreds of people to encounter Jesus and heal from their past.

When they're not traveling to see family and friends, Chuck and Marianne live in Boston, Massachusetts. Besides enjoying coffee dates, cross-fit, shopping, and a life rich with connection, they love "hanging out" with their six grandkids.